Wherefore comfort yourselves together, and edify one another, even as also ye do.

1 Thessalonians 5:11

Seeing Faith

by

Randall Franks

One of America's favorite TV cops and country

entertainers shares encouraging perspectives

on life and faith.

Peach Picked Publishing ISBN: 978-0-9849108-9-2
P.O. Box 42, Tunnel Hill, Georgia 30755
Column Editor: Rachel Brown Kirkland
Preliminary Column Editors: Stan Guess and Kevin Cummings
Photos unless otherwise noted © Randall Franks Media
Cover Photos: © *2020 Randall Franks Media*
Location: Dunlap Merchantile, Dunlap, Tenn. www.DunlapMercantile.com
A portion of the proceeds from this book will be donated
to the Share America Foundation, Inc.
www.shareamericafoundation.org

Dedicated to

The Lady Who Came and Said
"God Told Me 'You Are to Be a Preacher'"

The Preachers Who Have Touched My Life

The Men and Women of God in My Family Tree
Since Christ Was Resurrected

CONTRIBUTING PASTORS

CARROLL ALLEN
JEFF BROWN
CHRIS BRYANT
JAMIE ELLIS
JUSTIN GAZAWAY
DAVID SAMPSON
MIKE SMITH

Seeing Faith

Seeing Faith

Randall Franks

Seeing Faith

Forward

I pray that something within these pages inspires you to a closer walk with Jesus Christ.

Unlike many of my ancestors, the path God revealed for

Constantine

me was not as a pastor. Although he did place many within my family tree who played a role in the spreading of the gospel.

Whether they were men of rule, who decided upon the faith of their subjects like Emperor Constantine the Great of Rome, a pastor or deacon of a small rural church like Rev. Robert Shields, Jr., a circuit riding preacher, or a Lutheran theologian with a major ministry of missions such as Augustus Hermann Francke, my grandfathers facilitated the objective of the great commission.

As I prepare these pages for your reading, I am ever mindful that I am not a minister of the gospel. I am not a studied theologian. That is one of the reasons, I reached out and partnered

Francke

with those that are. You will find several pastors who invested their time in making the enclosed lessons a greater blessing to your study. Thank you to all these men who assisted me in making this study more impactful.

Shields

Thanks to their gracious donation of expertise, I will donate a portion of the sales of this book to benefit the Share America Foundation, Inc. which provides the Pearl and Floyd Franks

Seeing Faith

Scholarship for Appalachian youth in music.

As a singer and musician, I have stood in pulpits across the United States and Canada sharing the gospel in song. I have prayed for and with others. I have served His people. I have seen people saved and I have watched lives changed through their love of Jesus.

You may not know Him, but if you take the time to See Faith as I have, you may ask Him into your life or find that a closer walk with Him will bring you and Jesus on the same path. While walking together you may find the conversation within your soul enlightening. You may find the opportunities to serve others abounding. You may find Jesus is all you needed all along. You may find your way home to Him.

May "Seeing Faith" the way I have experienced it, be an open door unto or strengthen your walk with Jesus.

This devotional utilizes the King James Version of the Bible.

The author is a cousin to King James VI of Scotland and I of England who ordered the creation of the KJV Bible in 1604.

Seeing Faith
Truth, Nothing But the Truth

The importance of truth in everyday life is something that each of us are responsible for upholding.

When thinking on the topic of honesty, I fondly remember back on "The Andy Griffith Show" episode where Opie wants to sell his bike without mentioning all the little things that are wrong with it. Barney decides to take on selling real estate and the Taylors are considering selling their house and buying another in the same episode.

Andy neglects to mention the little odds and ends wrong with the house until Opie brings these things to the attention of the buyers. While Andy becomes frustrated by Opie's honesty, Opie is confused by Andy's separate rules for adults and children. Andy finally realizes that Opie is right.

When we are in our late teens, we sometimes add a few years to our age so we can do things adults do. As we get older, we tend to shave years off our age so we can appear younger. Are these lies?

When attorneys are faced with defending people that they know or suspect are guilty, does this strain their ability to be honest when they stand in front of a judge or jury to defend a not guilty plea?

While extreme situations like war can sometimes bring on the need for good people to be faced with challenging choices concerning their convictions, it is often on faith and truth that they must rely to get through the bad times. But there are, no doubt, times when honesty may be strained.

Seeing Faith

Members of a generation of Americans were disenfranchised by the feeling that our government was lying to them in the 1970s during Watergate and the latter part of the Vietnam War.

Were they lying?

There is an old joke about how you can tell when a politician is lying — their mouth is moving.

I wonder sometimes what happened to good, old-fashioned honesty.

Honesty does exist in each of us. All we need to do is remember each and every falsehood we utter has an effect on someone else.

It may only be ourselves we hurt as we build a house of cards trying to remember each and every white lie we have told so as not to be caught.

What is the point of being dishonest? Do we gain anything?

There's an old song called the "Royal Telephone" where the singer asks the operator to get Jesus on the line.

Would you tell a lie in exchange for a conversation with our Savior, Jesus Christ himself, on the phone? I wouldn't.

If I did, what would we talk about?

Remember: "From your lips to God's ears."

If you remember that he is listening, it does make you think more heavily about what you do and say each and every day.

Seeing Faith

Proverbs 12:22
"Lying lips are an abomination to the Lord:
but they that deal truly are his delight."

In "Truth, Nothing But the Truth" we see some of the moral struggles towards honesty that folks experience while trying to live our everyday lives. It challenges us to remember our accountability to God in being truthful to Him and to all of His children.

The message reflects this scriptural principle by highlighting the importance of upholding honesty and truthfulness in our everyday lives and interactions. It acknowledges the temptations and rationalizations that can lead people to stray from complete truthfulness, whether through seemingly harmless "white lies," selective omissions, or more serious deceptions. However, the overarching message aligns with Proverbs 12:22 by advocating for a commitment to dealing truly and eschewing dishonesty, recognizing that lying is detestable to God. The examples of Opie's moral struggle in the Andy Griffith episode and the questioning of when honesty might be strained illustrate the real tensions we face in pursuing truthfulness consistently. Ultimately, the message challenges readers to remember God's omnis-

Seeing Faith

cience and our accountability to Him, posing the hypothetical of lying even during a conversation with Christ to underscore honesty's significance. This perspective of remaining truthful because God delights in those who deal truly, reflects the wisdom expressed in Proverbs 12:22.

1. In what areas of your life have you been tempted to compromise truthfulness, and how can remembering this scripture help strengthen your commitment to honesty?

_____

_____

_____

_____

_____

2. How can we navigate situations where full truthfulness may seem to conflict with other ethical considerations, such as protecting someone's privacy or well being?

_____

_____

_____

_____

_____

Seeing Faith

3. Beyond simply avoiding overt lies, what are practical ways we can cultivate a lifestyle of truthfulness that pleases God, as this proverb encourages?

_____

_____

_____

_____

_____

Seeing Faith

Notes

Seeing Faith
Has a Lack of Faith Hurt America?

When our founding fathers got together to deliberate our future, they saw America as a land in which God could flourish, a bountiful land where people could be free to worship God, free from fear of reprisal from the government.

A review of their personal writings, the documents they created and the laws they made help support this idea. For centuries, humankind lived under rulers that decided how and whom they should worship.

In many cases, monarchs used religion to dictate what behavior they expected from their subjects. They would often change the precepts of a religion to suit their needs.

With the advent of Christianity, people from around the world were introduced to what would become the cornerstone of American culture. Out of one faith, many different viewpoints arose through the centuries, giving us a wide variety of religious denominations under one God.

It was these differences in faith and the desire to worship without persecution that brought the original settlers to these shores.

We can disagree about the particulars of how we worship, but all Christians can agree that we believe in God.

I think our forefathers never saw that the potential of the religious freedom they were creating would one day limit the growth of faith in America. The Judeo-Christian ethic upon which this land was built created the greatest society in history. Of course, other countries and leaders in history might disagree.

Seeing Faith

Many early settlers and leaders saw Christianity as the only religion. Missionaries in the east tried to convert Native Americans away from their beliefs to Christianity. The same holds true for Spanish missionaries in the southwest. American history reflects through laws and deeds a disdain for the occult. Suspected witches went through trials and were executed. These incidents preceded the establishment of rights outlined by our forefathers.

In many of the colonies, being a Christian was a prerequisite for office.

While our Constitution set forth that religious preferences would not be a factor in being elected to office, many states maintained being a Godly man as a prerequisite to hold political office.

Courtesy Library of Congress

Adams

No matter how you review the early history of our great land, the importance many of our founding fathers placed on belief in God is readily apparent.

President John Quincy Adams's father President John Adams was on the committee that wrote the Declaration. He stated in a speech given in the Town of Newburyport honoring the 61st anniversary of the Declaration of Independence that "The birthday of the nation is indissolubly linked with the birthday of the Saviour.... The Declaration of Independence first organized the social compact on the foundation of the Redeemer's mission upon earth (and) laid the cornerstone of human government upon the first precepts of Christianity."

In the last six decades, our courts and our legislatures

Seeing Faith

have rebuilt America to reflect the opinion of a few. "Separation of church and state" was never part of our Constitution. The First Amendment says that "Congress shall make no law respecting an establishment of religion, or prohibiting the free exercise thereof."

The emphasis is on the word "law."

While some lawmakers and upholders advocated that government should not define a particular religion, the words "separation of church and state" were not introduced

Courtesy Library of Congress

Jefferson

until 1802 by President Thomas Jefferson in a letter to the Danbury Baptist Association.

Since that time, our courts have used those words over and over again.

The words of the Constitution protect all religions from governments creating laws against them. Our Congress even endorsed by resolution the printing of Robert Aitken's Bible in 1782, the first English language Bible published in America.

It does not, however, preclude religious leaders, members of various religious faiths, Christian or otherwise, from having an effect upon government.

We have to remember that when these words were written the primary religion in our country was Christianity. Discussions about different religions usually applied to variations on the Christian faith, not on Buddhism, Hinduism, Muslimism, etc.

We are a "government by the people." I believe most religions are made up of people.

"Separation of Church and State" was supposed to pro-

Seeing Faith

tect religion from government, not prevent religious influences and concepts being part of government. A government reflects the people who participate by voting, taking office and voicing concerns through their elected officials.

They created a passage in our Constitution which prevented the state from interfering in the church, and encouraged our churches to be involved in government.

At the time, they unofficially recognized Christianity as the dominant religion of our nation through the inclusion of God, and their faith in God in so many of our documents.

Our early education system helped to instill the fundamentals of Christian morals to the youth of America. Many of the earliest communities held church and school in the same building.

Whether you believe religion should be a part of our public schools or not, since Christian teachings were removed, I think many will agree America and our youth are the losers.

I'm not knocking our schools. They do more than is sometimes apparently possible with what they are given. But without a moral compass, where does our future lie?

You might say people should get their morals at church or at home. What happens when they do not?

With the political correctness movement, government organizations tend to go far beyond the suggestions of the law to protect themselves from possible trouble, thus restricting religious freedoms.

This is exactly what our founding fathers wished to prevent. I think we are getting tied up in particulars. Should we have school-led prayer? Should the Ten Commandments hang on a courtroom wall? These are debates

Seeing Faith

that could go on endlessly.

To form my opinion, I look to these words from Patrick Henry and hope others might as well.

"It cannot be emphasized too strongly or too often that this great nation was founded, not by religionists, but by

Patrick Henry delivers a speech before the Virginia House of Burgesses against the Stamp Act of 1765.
(Engraver: Alfred Jones; Artist: Peter Rothermel — Courtesy Library of Congress)

Seeing Faith

Christians, not on religions, but on the gospel of Jesus Christ! For this very reason, peoples of other faiths have been afforded asylum, prosperity and freedom of worship here."

The author is a cousin to Presidents Thomas Jefferson, John Adams, John Quincy Adams and Patrick Henry referenced above.

Seeing Faith

Galatians 3:11
But that no man is justified by the law in the sight of God, it is evident: for, The just shall live by faith.

"Has a Lack of Faith Hurt America?" argues that America was founded on Christian principles and faith in God by the nation's founders, who envisioned religious freedom to worship God without government persecution. It expresses concern that in recent decades, an application of "separation of church and state" has been applied to remove religious influences from government and public spheres, contrary to the founders' intent. This resonates with the scripture Galatians 3:11 which states, "The just shall live by faith."

1. Have you personally believed on Christ as your Savior?

_____

_____

_____

_____

_____

Seeing Faith

2. Did you realize that the Separation of Church and State was enshrined into our social fabric to prevent the government from presiding over matters of faith within the Church of Christ?

_____
_____
_____
_____
_____

3. Do you believe that Christians should have an active role in influencing our government?

_____
_____
_____
_____
_____

Pastor Justin Gazaway
Catoosa Baptist Tabernacle in Ringgold, Ga.

Seeing Faith

It Is Hard to Walk Away When You Are at the Bottom of the Pile

Summer should be a time of wonder.

I remember fondly my childhood summers. Endless hours of play after completing my chores around the house. Of course, as I got older, I took on odd jobs like mowing neighbors' yards to earn a little money.

In my neighborhood, we had a great group of children. We all would gather to play and race our bikes down suicide hill. I remember one accident that sent me flying through the handle bars and sliding down the pavement for 20 feet or more. That still hurts just thinking about it. I had sores all over me from that adventure.

We would get in our share of disagreements with each other. That would lead usually to some hurt feelings and some rolling around on the ground till someone would say "uncle." We always seemed to come through it. There really were no children who caused trouble in my age bracket. A few older ones sometimes got into mischief, but we always managed to keep out of trouble.

Do not get me wrong — there were bullies. We were just blessed not to have them on our street, at least for very long. I remember when I was about seven there were two brothers who took great pleasure in picking fights with me. At least, it seemed that way at the time.

A boy my age named Chris Sands moved in. His parents had just divorced, and at that time it was not as usual as it is now. I'll never forget one meeting with those brothers which had me at the bottom of a wrestling match that I just

Seeing Faith

could not win. Chris was the new guy in the neighborhood and saw that I was being unfairly targeted for this fight and stepped in to pull the other boys off me. From that moment

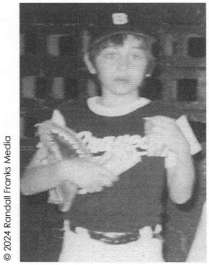

Chris Sands

on, he was my friend — that is until he later moved away, and I lost track of him.

While time has erased many of the memories of the time we spent together hanging out as kids, that one action by the new boy on the block sticks in my mind. He saw something that was not right, and he did something about it. Not knowing the social lay of the land and the dynamics of the neighborhood hierarchy, he stuck his neck out for me. That is bravery. It's not the Alvin York kind of bravery, or maybe it is. When Alvin saw his friends being hurt by the Germans, he moved into action to stop them from being hurt.

Now I'm not advocating fighting as a way to resolve issues for children or adults. I was taught that it takes much more courage to walk away than to actually fight. But when they jump on you, there are just a few hurdles you have to get over before you can walk away.

I learned a valuable lesson from Chris that day.

Folks often do not like to stick their neck out to help other people, but when someone does, it makes our community a better place.

Seeing Faith

Galatians 6:1-3
1 Brethren, if a man be overtaken in a fault, ye which are spiritual, restore such an one in the spirit of meekness; considering thyself, lest thou also be tempted.
2 Bear ye one another's burdens, and so fulfil the law of Christ.
3 For if a man think himself to be something, when he is nothing, he deceiveth himself.

As we born again believers live out our Christian walk, we ought to attempt to carefully tread that narrow way that Jesus spoke about. But the fact of the matter is that our flesh is not yet perfected, and sometimes, while walking on that narrow way we are going to fall down. Perhaps we fly over the handlebars. It may be that we have disagreements with one another. We might even find ourselves stuck on the bottom of the pile with seemingly no way out. In fact, our Bible tells us that, If we say that we have no sin, we deceive ourselves, and the truth is not in us (1 John 1:8). We might just have a period of time in our lives where our knees are scraped, our feelings bruised, and we just cannot see how to get back up again.

But no matter how many times we fall, or how bleak it looks, our Bible tells us that "a just man falleth seven times, and riseth up again." In the book of Galatians, the

Seeing Faith

Apostle Paul tells us that the "brethren," the born again believers which are spiritual, ought to restore that man that is taken in a fault, the man that is, perhaps, on the bottom of the pile. Beloved, our Lord expects us to be someone else's "Chris Sands."

1. Can you recall a situation where a brethren on that narrow way fell? What was your reaction? Did you pile on them or did you seek restoration?

_____

_____

_____

_____

_____

2. What do you suppose was the driving force behind your reaction to the aforementioned situation?

_____

_____

_____

_____

_____

Seeing Faith

3. How do you think our reaction to someone "on the bottom of the pile" reflects upon our relationship with the Lord?

_____

_____

_____

_____

_____

Assistant Pastor Mike Smith
Valley View Baptist Church in Flintstone, Georgia

Seeing Faith

Notes

Seeing Faith

A Little Soap and Water
Never Hurt Anyone

Bathing should not be an acquired taste.

Have you ever been sitting around and realized that there was an odor in your proximity? After close examination of your surroundings you came to the conclusion that no animals had crawled up under your chair and died, so there could only be one answer. Your Right Guard has done left.

There is an old joke about taking a bath once a week whether you need it or not.

I know as a child many of us dreaded the word "bath." That meant being covered in soap, washing behind your ears and quite a few other things. In many cases you would think we were distantly related to the wicked witch of the west, afraid that we would simply melt away from the face of the earth if water ever touched our body. Being dirty was just synonymous with being a kid.

Many of my summers growing up were spent on my grandparents farm. While Bill and Kitty did have running water, inside plumbing was not a convenience they had yet added when I was little.

They bathed much in the same way folks had done for centuries before the advent of modern plumbing — either in the creek that ran through the farm or by heating the water on the fire and pouring it into a bathing tub which was set strategically in one of the rooms in the house.

Queens and kings bathed this way. Often times I have read they bathed with less frequency during the cold harsh winters fearing the onset of some life threatening ailment. I

Seeing Faith

understand they had very strong perfume back then.

I remember watching "The Beverly Hillbillies" with delight as one of the characters sat soapy in one of those tubs in the middle of the kitchen or courting parlor as Granny poured hot water over them. I guess while many Americans who enjoyed modern conveniences found that funny or quaint, personally, I related with it because I had done the same thing. I knew that was reality.

Baths were always a Saturday adventure at my grandparents'. In the summer because it was usually so hot inside, baths were taken outside. It wasn't like anybody was going to see you way out in the country. The nearest neighbor was better than a couple of miles off as the crow flies. Besides, most of them were busy doing the same thing.

A section of the back porch was dedicated for the washtub, and whether you needed it or not, you were doused with water heated from an open fire. The soap was homemade, lye I believe. And that scrub brush could have been used to scrape paint off the side of the house. At least, that is the way it seemed to a kid in a hurry to get back to putting the dirt on. Of course, the men and women folk had run of the bathing area at different times.

Now this weekly ritual does not mean that cleaning did not occur at other points in the week. Most days folks washed with a rag over the wash basin with a pitcher. It was just on Saturday you got the whole works done at once.

While many wax nostalgic about the good old days, I am proud that these are some experiences that I shared with my ancestors. I'm afraid in our world of modern convenience where we no longer have to carry water from the creek or

Seeing Faith

well to wash ourselves or our clothes, sometimes we forget just how far we have come in such a short time.

Today, with the turn of a handle, most of us have all the water we need — cold or hot. We can stand underneath a good, hot shower and cleanse away the grit and grime we pick up along life's way.

For most, there is no reason not to remember the old saying "cleanliness is next to Godliness."

If we do, maybe when we get to Heaven, Saint Peter will be less likely to turn us away. I bet there are not that many perfume or deodorant stores up there. 'Course, I bet by now Sam Walton has probably opened a Walmart. You can get anything there.

Proverbs 22:6
Train up a child in the way he should go: and when
he is old, he will not depart from it.

The nostalgic reflection on the weekly bathing ritual
from the writer's youth demonstrates the scriptural exhortation in Proverbs 22:6 to diligently train children in proper
ways from an early age. Though the bathing methods seem
antiquated today, the message shows how basic hygiene
habits were ingrained through this family tradition passed
down from previous generations. The practices of heating
water, using homemade lye soap, and thoroughly scrubbing
on Saturday baths became formative experiences that
shaped the writer's lifelong value of cleanliness — a virtue
viewed as being next to godliness. By recounting these
childhood memories, the message highlights how participating in such intentional training left an indelible mark
and reinforced principles the writer still holds dear. This
underscores the wisdom in Proverbs 22:6, that the ways
children are trained in their youth will stick with them into
adulthood, for better or worse. The bathing vignettes provide a tangible example of putting this biblical parenting
guidance into practice.

Seeing Faith

1. Why is bathing the body part of "training a child in the way he should go."

_____

_____

_____

_____

_____

2. Some Catholics believe if they have a child until the age of seven, he (she) will be a Catholic for life. How can the present day church survive without training it's present generation?

_____

_____

_____

_____

_____

Seeing Faith

3. When did Jesus use water for cleaning, or to represent spiritual cleansing?

_____

_____

_____

_____

_____

Seeing Faith
The Show Must Go On

People are often impressed by the glamour they think makes up such a large portion of stars' lives.

As I drove into the McReynolds' farm outside Nashville, in my mind I was preparing for another weekend out on the road with Grand Ole Opry stars Jim and Jesse. Jesse and his late wife Darlene opened their home to me, and I often stayed overnight in the two-story farmhouse where they raised their family. When the brothers joined the Opry, they bought a farm which they both lived on.

Grand Ole Opry stars Jim and Jesse McReynolds review a script at WCYB-TV Bristol, Virginia in 1993.

In many ways, I became an extended member of the family. When I drove into the driveway, I noticed the back of the bus opened up. Underneath the bus, I found Jesse tangled between what makes a diesel engine tick. Folks who are use to seeing stars with their hair slicked back in the sparkling stage attire would not have recognized this Bluegrass Hall of Famer as he climbed from beneath the bus in his ragged baseball cap and gray coveralls covered with grease. Jesse

Seeing Faith

was a mechanical whiz.

The duo often worked with Country Music Hall of Famer Charlie Louvin. Charlie and I became acquainted while I was still in my teens. I remember one time he and I sat down and discussed the merits of a career in music. He told me then that he had spent most of his life working for a bus and a band. Keeping those two things on the road had taken most of what he made. He reflected on an early decision to select music over a job at the post office. At the time he said if he had taken that post office job, he would be retired and drawing a pension now. I spoke with him after he and his late brother Ira's induction in the hall of fame. I know if he had made the other choice it would have been a great loss to the world, but it goes to show that even stars sometimes wonder about their life choices.

Concert goers don't often realize what is involved in putting on a stage show. The performers in many cases gather at their home base and load the bus or van with equipment, sales material, personal effects and enough snack food to tide them through the trip. It is not unusual to climb aboard and ride for 10 to 12 hours to the venue. After arriving, they figure out where things go and then unload sound equipment and sales material. After setting everything up for the arrival of the audience, performers then go and throw a little water on their face, slick back their hair and put on their stage clothes.

We arrived somewhere in Ohio, Bellevue, I think. Members of Jim and Jesse's band, the Virginia Boys, and I had went through the set-up process with Georgia Music Hall of Famers, the Lewis Family, who were sharing the bill that

Seeing Faith

Randall Franks on stage sharing some dialogue with Jim McReynolds as they and the Lewis Family prepare to perform a song together in the 1990s.

night. Everything was set, and we were all ready to go on. I was standing backstage waiting anxiously as Jim and Jesse went through their first set. They would usually bring me on about 10 to 15 minutes into the show. The Lewis Family's sound equipment was on the stage. I don't remember the exact conversation that led up to it, but Travis Lewis, who usually watched the controls, and I were joking backstage. I said, "It is liable to blow when I go out there."

As the audience laughed at my first punch line, I hit the first chord. The sound system blew. I was standing there with some of America's most talented musicians ready to play and no way for the audience to hear us. Thanks to the fast work of Travis, Little Roy Lewis and a couple of others, they got the system up and running. Needless to say for any entertainer, standing in front of audience, and trying to

Seeing Faith

keep them entertained as the sound system is being fixed is less than a glamorous situation.

When the show is over, after visiting with the folks in the audience, the groups have to tear down the equipment, load up, and hit the road for the next gig and do it all over again.

What I have found through the years is that stars who tend to take care of things themselves have the longest and most productive careers.

I'd rather be more like Jesse, putting on the grease covered coveralls to keep things going than having everything served on a silver platter.

But I'll never joke about blowing out the sound system again. You don't reckon it was my singing do you?

Seeing Faith
STUDY ONE

Psalm 34:15
The eyes of the LORD are upon the righteous, and his ears are open unto their cry.

Proverbs 15:3
The eyes of the LORD are in every place, beholding the evil and the good.

Hebrews 6:10
For God is not unrighteous to forget your work and labour of love, which ye have shewed toward his name, in that ye have ministered to the saints, and do minister.

In the quiet moments of our lives, when the world may not be watching, we find ourselves echoing the humble example of Jesse McReynolds. It is often the case that our efforts and toils remain hidden from the worldly stage. Yet, we can take solace in the profound truth that there is One who beholds our every endeavor. His gaze transcends the limitations of mortal vision. His attention never wavers or strays from our side. This One is none other than the Lord Jesus Christ, the Sovereign Lord of all creation.

As the Psalmist so beautifully declared, "The eyes of the LORD are upon the righteous, and His ears are open unto

Seeing Faith

their cry" (Psalm 34:15). In these words, we find both comfort and conviction. We are assured that our labor is not in vain, for the Lord watches over us with unfailing love. Our dedication and service are not for the fleeting applause of humanity but for the eternal and divine cause of Christ. Let us, therefore, continue to labor faithfully, knowing that our Lord's eyes are ever upon us and our work is eternally meaningful in His sight.

1. The message highlights the behind-the-scenes efforts and hard work required by musicians and performers, even those who have achieved success and fame. How does this relate to the biblical principle that God sees and values our labor, even when it may go unnoticed by the world, as expressed in Psalm 34:15 and Proverbs 15:3?

_____

_____

_____

_____

_____

Seeing Faith

2. The commentary emphasizes that our work and service should ultimately be for the "eternal and divine cause of Christ," rather than for fleeting human praise or recognition. How can we cultivate this mindset and keep our motivations focused on honoring God in our daily lives and vocations?

_____

_____

_____

_____

_____

3. Hebrews 6:10 assures us that God "is not unrighteous to forget" our work and labor of love. How can this promise encourage us to persevere in our efforts, even when facing challenges or setbacks, knowing that our service is ultimately seen and rewarded by God?

_____

_____

_____

_____

_____

Dr. David Sampson
Parkway Baptist in Fort Oglethorpe, Georgia

Seeing Faith

Proverbs 3:5-7
Trust in the LORD with all thine heart; and lean not unto thine own understanding. In all thy ways acknowledge him, and he shall direct thy paths. Be not wise in thine own eyes: fear the LORD, and depart from evil.

Ephesians 5:15-16
See then that ye walk circumspectly, not as fools, but as wise, Redeeming the time, because the days are evil.

Proverbs 16:9
A man's heart deviseth his way: but the LORD directeth his steps.

STUDY TWO

In the grand tapestry of human existence, irrespective of our diverse backgrounds and varied stations in life, we are all inevitably presented with choices. These choices, seemingly ordinary and mundane in the present moment, carry profound implications for the trajectory of our lives. Hence, it is paramount to exercise discernment and wisdom in our decision-making. Just as Charlie Louvin once stood at a crossroads and made a pivotal choice that indelibly altered the course of his life, our own choices possess the potential to etch a lasting imprint upon the annals of history, much

Seeing Faith

like Charlie's influence upon the world of country music. The writer of Proverbs said: "Trust in the LORD with all thine heart; and lean not unto thine own understanding. In all thy ways acknowledge him, and he shall direct thy paths. Be not wise in thine own eyes: fear the LORD, and depart from evil" (Proverbs 3:5-7). This passage of Scripture encourages us to cultivate a deep and abiding trust in God, to rely on His wisdom over our own understanding, and to seek His guidance in every aspect of our lives. By doing so, we acknowledge His sovereignty, and in return, He promises to guide us along the path of life. When we trust in the Lord, lean on His wisdom, and acknowledge Him in all we do, we open ourselves to His divine guidance. Living the Christian life does not necessarily entail leading a trouble-free life but rather a life guided by His wisdom and the comfort of His presence.

1. The message highlights the hard work, dedication, and sometimes unglamorous realities behind the careers of successful musicians like Jesse McReynolds and Charlie Louvin. How does this relate to the biblical principle found in Ephesians 5:15-16 about walking wisely and redeeming the time, even in the midst of challenging circumstances?

_____

_____

_____

_____

_____

Seeing Faith

2. The commentary emphasizes the importance of trusting in the Lord's guidance and acknowledging Him in all our ways, as instructed in Proverbs 3:5-7. How can we apply this principle to major life decisions, such as the choice between different career paths, as Charlie Louvin faced?

_____

_____

_____

_____

_____

3. Proverbs 16:9 states that while a person may devise their own way; it is ultimately the Lord who directs their steps. How can this truth provide comfort and assurance, even when we face setbacks or unforeseen circumstances, like the sound system malfunction described in the message?

_____

_____

_____

_____

_____

Dr. David Sampson
Parkway Baptist in Fort Oglethorpe, Georgia

Seeing Faith
Will I Find It?

There are times I find myself looking for something that had eluded me.

In childhood, one of my favorite Saturday morning shows was "The Land of the Lost."

In the story line, humans fell through a crack in space and time to the period and place where they had to exist with dinosaurs.

I am not sure where that crack is they fell through. I have never seen it but I have a feeling that it simply appears and disappears at will.

I currently have a line of socks sitting on my ironing board with no mates.

The crack seems to be drawn to my dryer. While I generally have liked wearing matching socks, I am beginning to think that trend will have to change in order to stay ahead of the losses.

Perhaps it has a magnetism, the crack simply appears when something desires to escape its surroundings and find new adventures.

I don't know where those little items get to that seem to take the trip.

Eventually, though they find their way back and usually just slightly off from their original position no worse for the wear.

I imagine though some of them could write a book that only the other inanimate objects could appreciate.

I have often placed the disappearances especially on items like car keys or things which delay departure as sim-

Seeing Faith

ply an angelical nudge to prevent some unknown course of action which would not have been in my best interest.

Even those times pass as the item reveals itself and the original desired departure occurs.

Sometimes I wonder if they are lost or are we. Are we searching in vain in this world trying to find something that we do not really need?

Is the path that is promised that is ahead what we have really lost?

As we look upon recent events both here at home and abroad, sometimes I feel that we all have now fallen through that crack into the land of the lost. It seems that the dinosaurs have taken a different form but they still put our future at peril.

In the increasing sequence of velocity of the negative, I am pleased to see through the crack the reverberations of those who are seeking the Light of God's love, being drawn into Revival at points reaching out initially from the crack that revealed itself at Asbury University in Kentucky in 2023.

Perhaps this crack will widen and allow many more of the Lost to be found, perhaps the socks will find their match, the keys will reappear with destination fully ready to receive all those with a willing heart.

May our land become the center of such rejoicing in God's gifts that no one resides in the land of the lost.

Seeing Faith

Luke 15:8-9
Either what woman having ten pieces of silver, if she lose one piece, doth not light a candle, and sweep the house, and seek diligently till she find it?
And when she hath found it, she calleth her friends and her neighbours together, saying, Rejoice with me; for I have found the piece which I had lost.

The God of the gospel of Jesus Christ is a finder of lost things. We often speak of terms of "finding God" but truthfully, it's the other way around. If we have the right-kind-of eyes we might find ourselves surprised by all the things we can see God bringing to light. At the very least, let's rejoice with others who are seeing such.

1. How does the woman's joy upon finding the lost coin mirror God's joy when a lost soul is found?

_____

_____

_____

_____

_____

Seeing Faith

2. In what ways can we actively participate in God's mission to seek and save the lost, as depicted in this parable?

_____

_____

_____

_____

_____

3. What does this parable reveal about the importance of community and celebration in the context of spiritual restoration?

_____

_____

_____

_____

_____

Pastor Chris Bryant
Ringgold United Methodist Chuch of Ringgold, Georgia

Seeing Faith
The Spirit Within

Have you ever been in a room, and someone walks in and with your body you feel in your center mass of your chest a quiver.

As they draw closer to you, the disturbance within increases in its frequency of movement. Of course, exposing this in a public situation would be uncomfortable, so instead you hold your composure and let it pass. Hopefully, the situation does not place the person in your orbit.

I have experienced this and over the years as I moved on with my life, where I had the opportunity have watched those that the quiver warned me about. I have surmised that the Spirit within me was warning me that there was something within that person that was not coming from a good place, and they did not intend the best through their actions.

There have been occasions when such a person did come into my orbit, and it was all that I could do to withstand the impact of that exposure.

I have had similar experiences while seeing people on the news or while watching a TV show or a movie.

This feeling is much like a magnet when it pushes the same pole end apart. It's there to warn us to protect ourselves against the evil around us.

That comes in many packages, sometimes with legs, sometimes through what we watch, hear, read, and see. If you intake things that uplift your Spirit, reinforce it and feed it with positive, uplifting messages, love for your fellow man, then that will be reflected in the actions of your heart.

Seeing Faith

If you allow things that damage your Spirit, that expose you to darkness, evil, sadness, then your Spirit hardens and the warning quiver fades because you have in essence chosen to ignore it, then your actions will more and more reflect those negatives that you allow to invade your body. When I have not ignored its warnings, that Spirit has guided me safely through much of my life.

Although like any headstrong child — of any age — during some periods and on some days, I have lost my way, giving in to other senses and feelings allowing those to overshadow the Spirit. That has always been to my detriment, emotionally, sometimes physically and financially.

When it occurs, it weakens my Spirit, depletes my energy and scatters my focus. It saddens me when I realize that I stepped outside the blessings my companion offers.

I believe that the Spirit is God's way to be present in our lives and to walk with us in all that we do. When we ignore it, we are choosing to follow our own will, which is a choice that He gave us. Sometimes though when we follow the Pied Piper down the path, at some point we will have to pay the piper. Our hope then must be that if we choose to walk another path that it does not lead to our destruction or into the total hardening of the Spirit within us, so we no longer recognize ourselves.

Let's fill our minds, our hearts, our eyes, our ears with the uplifting Word and with images, stories, films and TV shows, that reinforce the good within us. Let's cast off that which is meant to draw us into a downward spiral with some aspect of destruction inevitable.

Seeing Faith

1 Thessalonians 5:19-22
Quench not the Spirit.
Despise not prophesyings,
Prove all things; hold fast that which is good.
Abstain from all appearance of evil.

Sometimes the space between the natural and the super-natural gets thin and we can "feel" it within us. Of course, God is both the God of the natural and the supernatural so we shouldn't be surprised that often through very everyday things we can sense something more that just what is there or what is happening. Indeed, there is a "spirit" to many things and people, but is it the Holy Spirit?

1. What practical steps can we take to effectively test everything and hold fast to what is good?

_____

_____

_____

_____

_____

Seeing Faith

2. How can we distinguish between "good" and "evil" in various situations as we read in verse 22.

_____

_____

_____

_____

_____

3. What practices or habits can help us abstain from every form of evil in our lives?

_____

_____

_____

_____

_____

Pastor Chris Bryant
Ringgold United Methodist Chuch of Ringgold, Georgia

Seeing Faith
The Miracle of a Migraine

With each passing year, all of us have dates that we mark in our minds or hearts as important.

As I reach the end of August each year my thoughts reflect on the last days of my late father, Floyd, who passed on Aug. 30, 1987.

In his last days, Dad faced a fierce but short battle with lung cancer. Years of smoking had led him into a skirmish I know he did not want to face at the young age of 54.

On Aug. 29, I arose early to take a school exam. Upon returning from school my father asked me to drive him

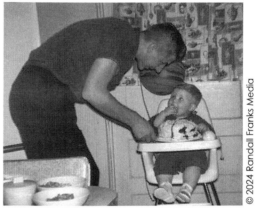

Floyd Franks helps his son Randall get a piece of his first birthday cake.

about 30 miles away to look at a used riding lawnmower.

It had been just six weeks since he had been diagnosed. They told him if treatments were successful he could have five years more to share with us. As with most people who undergo chemotherapy, he experienced a rough six weeks. His once perfect hair, which as a child I had so many times seen him carefully take his black comb from his pocket and straighten the ridge at the front of his head, now was gone and his body was almost a shell of the strong man I had grown to love and depend on in so many ways.

Seeing Faith

Dad used the trip for the lawnmower to tell me how proud he was of me and shared some hopes for my future. We drove and I listened.

He said that he enjoyed the years of helping me as road manager as I traveled on the road playing music. He and Mom took care of the countless details which were needed out there that we never even knew about.

I wish I could remember every word, but I can't. Perhaps in many ways I was trying to block what he said because in my heart I knew this was his way of telling me goodbye.

Floyd and Pearl Franks

I do not know how he knew his time was nearing. I later found out he had spent much of the previous day doing the same with my Mom. He was anxiously awaiting the arrival of my brother, who lived out of town, so he could also speak with him.

We checked out the mower and of course we did not buy it. We went on our way back to the house.

Upon returning, I prepared to leave for a show. I was performing at the annual Gospel Gold Festival with the Marksmen Quartet in Dahlonega.

We did our show around 7 p.m., then I visited with folks around the record table signing a few autographs. The Florida Boys, one of my early TV heroes, were scheduled

Seeing Faith

to perform at 10 p.m., so I was going to wait to see them for the first time in person.

As I sat at the table, I began to develop a tremendous migraine. As nausea set in, I knew I had to leave and make the two-hour drive back home.

I turned to the Marksmen leader, Earle Wheeler, and said "I've got to go now. If I don't, I will not be able to make it."

The symptoms progressively got worse on the trip home, but I pressed on through the darkness.

As I pulled onto Warwick Circle, all the lights in my house were on. I rushed in to find nobody home. There was a note on the kitchen table from my mom, which said "Gone to Hospital." On the phone were two urgent messages from her. I jumped in my truck and rushed to the hospital.

Floyd and Randall Franks attend a Boy Scout Jamboree.

As I entered the hospital I was ushered quickly to the seventh floor. I saw a lady in the distance near the pay phone. I did not even recognize her as my mother. The weight of the circumstances were heavy on her shoulders.

My father insisted on spending his time not in a hospital room but in the patient's day room.

I arrived just in time to share my father's last hour before God called him home. Mom and I held his hands as he literally walked into that good night. And he did walk

Seeing Faith

straight into God's arms.

When I reached the door to our house earlier that evening, that headache and all the symptoms which had beckoned me home were gone.

I was sent a message to come home through God's telephone.

If God had not placed upon me that affliction, I would have stayed and enjoyed the show and would have missed being with my Dad in those final moments.

That migraine was a miracle to me that helped me to experience what life and death is really about; it's about the people we love and how we share our time together.

Pearl and Floyd Franks
Learn about their Share America scholarship at
www.ShareAmericaFoundation.org

Seeing Faith

Genesis 50:20
But as for you, ye thought evil against me; but God meant it unto good, to bring to pass, as it is this day, to save much people alive.

Romans 8:28
And we know that all things work together for good to them that love God, to them who are the called according to his purpose.

We must understand that our lives are like puzzles. God, being omniscient, sees every piece of the puzzle. However, we can only see a few pieces of the puzzle at one time. What we see as bad circumstances God sees as necessary pieces to create a beautiful masterpiece. What may seem evil to you now, may just be meant for good in the end.

Seeing Faith

1. Hindsight is 20/20. Considering the story of Randall's migraine headache, examine and reflect upon your own life. Are there times that God used what seemed like a bad situation to bring about a blessing in your own life?

_____

_____

_____

_____

_____

2. Are there times when you can remember being distracted or delayed only to realize later that there was an accident that took place where you might have been? Could God possibly have been the cause of the distraction or delay?

_____

_____

_____

_____

_____

Seeing Faith

3. Instead of complaining or being discouraged over bad circumstances in your life, have you considered possibly thanking God for what He might be trying to perform in your life? (1 Thessalonians 5:18) He is the potter and we are the clay. Remember that the vessel will never be formed without the fire.

_____

_____

_____

_____

_____

Pastor Jeff Brown
Valley View Baptist Church in Flintstone, Georgia

Seeing Faith

Support the Share America Foundation, Inc. by
ITunes downloads or donating for
these great recordings:
www.Share AmericaFoundation.org

Seeing Faith
Reaching Goals

Reaching lifetime goals often means it is time to refor-mulate your life and create new goals.

Three decades ago, I reached a goal I had pursued since I was a little child.

Randall Franks (right) with Earl Scruggs (center) and James Monroe in 1984 in Nashville

Since the first time I watched Lester Flatt and Earl Scruggs sing "Little Girl of Mine In Tennessee" to "Granny" and "Uncle Jed" on "The Beverly Hill-billies," since the first time I saw Wayne Newton play a down home country boy who could really saw the fiddle, or since the first time I watched Doug Dillard and all the Dillards entertain "Sheriff Andy Taylor" as "The Darlings" on the "Andy Griffith Show" with his up tempo banjo tunes, I dreamed of walking on net-work television to pick and grin.

I always figured that such national exposure for a young boy from Georgia had to come through music. There were just not that

Randall Franks with Doug Dillard in 1991 in Nashville

Seeing Faith

many other avenues at that time. So I worked and studied to improve my music, working to create and market our youth group, The Peachtree Pickers®, by working flea markets, churches and schools. We began competing at fiddlers' conventions and then moved up to entertaining larger and larger audiences at bluegrass festivals and fairs. The support of my parents and those of the other group members helped to move our joint goals forward. We reached network cable in its infancy with a children's show

Randall Franks (right) and Jerry Coursey perform on the set of "The Country Kids TV Series."

called "The Country Kids TV Series," essentially a children's "Hee Haw" which aired in the United States and abroad. Our growth would eventually lead us to performances for the Grand Ole Opry and some acceptance by the more mainstream music industry.

In 1987, members of our youth act decided to go their separate ways, partially due to new college obligations. I was at a new point in my life, trying to decide what is next.

I had not yet reached my childhood goal, but without a group, which was still the foundation of bluegrass and southern gospel music at that time, I did not know what my next step would be. I decided to make some solo appearances pulling together musicians when needed and continued appearing with other acts for which I moonlighted when our group was not working, such as The Marksmen

Seeing Faith

Quartet and Doodle and the Golden River Grass.

I began work at Atlanta-based Southern gospel music label MBM records in 1987 helping to guide the careers of several artists signed with the label while still performing every opportunity I had.

In 1988, the label changed hands and my job was eliminated. So, once again, I found myself searching. While I had enjoyed doing some minor acting in school, I decided in order to reach my television goal I would have to begin a more intensive study of acting and take any opportunity, which were not many at the time I could to get to be on screen in Georgia.

But God seemed to immediately open the doors, giving me opportunity after opportunity. The music talents God gave me seemed to put me where I needed to be. It would not be music that landed me my role as "Officer Randy Goode" on "In the Heat of the Night," but it would be the many friends I developed from years of touring and recording that would share their exuberance about my presence on the show. After countless requests from those who cared about my music asking for me to perform on the show, Carroll

© 1992 Randall Franks Media – J. Alan Palmer

Randall Franks (right) and Thomas Byrd on the set of "In the Heat of the Night" film "Random's Child."

Seeing Faith

O'Connor wrote a uniquely designed scene in an episode entitled "Random's Child" which would set up a reason and purpose for "Officer Randy" to be pickin' and grinnin' just to frustrate the bad guys in that episode. One of those bad guys was Robert O'Reilly, "Gowron," leader of the Klingons, from "Star Trek, Deep Space Nine." I bet that is the only time in my life I will get to aggravate a Klingon.

O'Connor

© 1990 Authy-Franks Prods./Ned D. Burris

Anyway, Carroll wrote a little piece entitled the "Sparta Blues" for actor Thomas Byrd and I to perform at the Sparta Police impound yard when the bad guys came to claim their car. With the technical coaching of guitarist John Farley, I created the musical piece to bring the words alive.

I have always jokingly called it my biggest hit since millions heard it Nov. 25, 1992, on CBS and millions more around the world have heard it since. I've often wondered what it sounded like when translated into Chinese or Italian. It took years but the childhood dream was reached, and the goal I had chased for years was accomplished.

Then I had to decide what was next. Life is a constant re-evaluation of where you are and where you are going. We can't just simply drift, or what service will that be to God and our fellow man? He has a purpose for everyone's life. It is up to us to make His vision for us happen. He will open the doors; we must simply study and be prepared to walk through. But at the same time, as we walk with the confidence He gave us, we must always be mindful of whether what we are reaching for is His will or one we have created. Only time will tell.

Seeing Faith

Jeremiah 29:11
For I know the thoughts that I think toward you, saith the LORD, thoughts of peace, and not of evil, to give you an expected end.

Psalm 37:23
The steps of a good man are ordered by the LORD: and he delighteth in his way.

Matthew 6:21
For where your treasure is, there will your heart be also.

Every one of us has a dream. Some dream of being policemen, doctors, firefighters, soldiers, teachers, preachers and even as in Randall Franks's case, entertainers. God does call and lead people into each one of these and many other professions that have not been mentioned here. However, there is a key to every goal that you may be reaching for. The key is that you must ensure that your personal goal is God's will for your life. Pursuing goals that are contrary to God's will only leads to hurt and heartache. God has a plan for you, but so does the enemy. Make sure you have chosen the right path. (Matthew 7:13)

Seeing Faith

1. What are some personal goals that you are currently reaching for?

_____

_____

_____

_____

2. Have you put much time and prayer into your choice of those goals and do those goals line up with Scripture?

_____

_____

_____

_____

_____

3. How will you feel if you fail to reach those goals? Could it possibly be that those were not God's goals for you to begin with?

_____

_____

_____

_____

_____

Pastor Jeff Brown
Valley View Baptist Church in Flintstone, Georgia

Seeing Faith
The Gift of Music

Have you ever watched a child cast one toy aside and reach for something else? A friend of mine once told me he had watched his grandchildren open gifts and cast each one aside looking for the next one while spending no time with the one they just opened. He shared with me that at that point he knew his grandchildren had come to expect too much, wanting more and more — rather than being satisfied with one gift, they wanted to rip through dozens and then simply cast them aside.

Randall's childhood spinet piano sits between his family living and dining rooms.

I looked at my watch as mother drove by the old Colonial Grocery Store saying, "Hurry, Mom, we are going to be late." Of course we were not going to be late. The piano store was just next door. I picked up my books and rushed inside. I was always amazed at a store filled with pianos — I really wanted to get there early so I could go through and try out several of them while I waited my turn with piano teacher Jean Stiles.

I do not know what made me want to go from instrument to instrument playing. Perhaps it was the same desire

73

Seeing Faith

that made those children my friend had described ripping through more and more presents, although the pianos were not mine and would not be.

I was intrigued by the talents of gospel pianist Hovie Lister, Eva Mae LeFevre and classical pianist Victor Borge. Several of my cousins had the knack to play piano along with their singing, so I had hoped the gene passed to me as well.

Hovie Lister appears on stage at the Colonnade in Ringgold, Georgia. in one of his final concerts in 2001.

Of course, as a child of eight, my repertoire was a bit slim. In spite of the best efforts of my teacher, I was not the most proficient student who worked through "The Minuet" and "The Entertainer."

Eva Mae LeFevre
and Randall Franks

No matter my deficiencies, I had a true desire and my mother supported that to no end. She worked overtime to afford a walnut Currier Spinet piano and pay for my lessons.

One day while sitting in my elementary school room, the entire course of

74

Seeing Faith

Grisier

my life changed. Dr. Donald Grisier, DeKalb County orchestra teacher, came into the room and played a tune popularized by Chubby Wise — Ervin Rouse's "Orange Blossom Special" on the violin. I have not been worth shooting since.

I had heard my great Uncle Tom Franks play the violin like his father A. J.

Tom Franks

Harve Franks had done before him at family gatherings, but now there was someone willing to sit and teach me.

After convincing my parents that I wanted to learn violin, I signed up. My mother once again went out of her way to see that I got the opportunity by renting an instrument. I also

Harve Franks

continued my piano study, but eventually it did fade away in the shadow of the fiddle. I realized I was not going to be the next Hovie Lister or Victor Borge. The fiddle would stick and lead me to some amazing places.

While I would never consider myself a pianist, the knowledge I gained while learning about the instrument has served me extremely well in every musical endeavor. The experience prepared me for a lifetime of lessons in almost every pursuit I've chosen to follow. Even playing along with Jeff & Sheri Easter on old TV shows.

So, while at times children may be spoiled by piles and piles of material gifts that simply get laid aside, if a child shows interest in music, even if the child has absolutely no

Seeing Faith

talent for it, and may someday lay the expensive instrument aside for other pursuits, remember as the child's practicing causes the paint to peel in the family room, love of music is a gift that will last a lifetime and can span the generations.

Seeing Faith

Psalm 98:4
"Make a joyful noise unto the Lord, all the earth:
make a loud noise, and rejoice, and sing praise."

"The Gift of Music" touches upon the importance of instilling a love of music from a young age. Teaching children to sing or play an instrument provides a perfect way for any of us to allow the next generation a lifetime of praising God through music.

The message reflects this scriptural exhortation to praise God through joyful music and singing. It recounts the author's childhood experiences of being exposed to and cultivating a love for various musical instruments, particularly the piano and violin. While acknowledging the potential for children to become unappreciative of material gifts, the message emphasizes the enduring value of nurturing an interest in music from a young age. The author's mother's sacrifice to provide piano lessons and a violin, despite limited means, aligns with the scriptural call to rejoice and sing praises unto the Lord. The message portrays music not merely as a pastime but as a lifelong gift that can span generations, echoing the psalmist's directive for all the earth to make a joyful noise unto God. The author's journey from

Seeing Faith

attempting to emulate accomplished musicians to ultimately finding his niche with the violin exemplifies the essence of using one's talents and passions to create joyful melodies that honor the Creator.

1. How has music played a role in your spiritual life and ability to worship God joyfully?

_____

_____

_____

_____

_____

2. In what ways can we encourage and nurture an appreciation for music, especially among younger generations, as a means of praising the Lord?

_____

_____

_____

_____

_____

Seeing Faith

3. Beyond musical instruments, what other God-given talents or creative outlets can we cultivate as expressions of joyful noise and praise?

_____

_____

_____

_____

_____

Seeing Faith

Notes

Seeing Faith
A Man's Word is His Bond

I have been told there was a time when a person was judged upon the words which emanated from his mouth.

A person's character could be seen in his deeds and by what he would say and sometimes what he would not say. I have met many people in my life. Some, I would not trust them as far as I could throw them, while others — if they say it, it will be done.

Bill

When two people struck a bargain and shook hands there was nothing else to do.

Today, however, we are in a world filled will reams of contracts, agreements and endless disclaimers and visits to a lawyer.

My Grandpa Bill was a man of his word. If he said he would help with something, no matter what hardship it placed upon him, he would do it.

In my association with music legend Bill Monroe, I learned quickly that his honor was paramount in his image.

Monroe

There was never a bargain struck or a promise made between he and I that he did not make come to pass.

I remember visiting with him before his final illness. He walked up to me and with the strength of a 20-year-old he squeezed my hand. He looked at me dead in the eye and said, "I tell you man, there are not that many good men left any more. Men like us need to stick together and help each other out."

More than his praise of my musical ability or all the

Seeing Faith

things he had done for me in my life, those few words conveyed to me that he thought of me as a man of my word. Working in the world of television and film, I quickly learned the lesson that many Hollywood movers and shakers tend to be the opposite. Most of these trendsetters simply tell you what you want to hear rather than the truth.

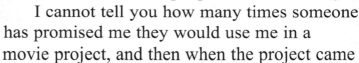

This trend relates more to the stars and executives of the last two to three decades.

There are and were what I call "class acts" such as the late stars Gene Autry, John Wayne and Roy Rogers whose word was their bond. I wish there were more people like them today.

I cannot tell you how many times someone has promised me they would use me in a

Rogers

movie project, and then when the project came along that promise was forgotten.

I am afraid I have found the same to be true in the "real" world as well.

Sometimes it just makes you want to lose faith in the entire human race when a person tells you he will do one thing and he does another.

In my own life, I have never broken a promise or not followed through with an agreement. Being a man of your word also carries through to fulfilling the everyday tasks that we all do. Returning phone calls, fulfilling requests, replying to mail are just a few of the little things that some folks might miss. I know that I have probably misstepped by not doing a few things that I have said I would do in my life. For those touched by such an action, I ask for forgiveness.

Seeing Faith

But I also know when I have told someone I would do something, usually such an assurance has popped up in my memory over and over again until I finish the task. There have been times I have carried one of those little things around in my head for a couple of years until I could do something about it.

But no matter what, I always did it.

Despite trends to the contrary and those who we discover are not honorable by their deeds and words, I believe it is the responsibility of every individual to make every effort to rise above such people to make our community a place of honor. It is what we owe our forefathers who built this land, and what we owe those who fight and die for our continued freedom.

Seeing Faith

1 John 2:4
He that saith, I know Him, and keepeth not his commandments, is a liar, and the truth is not in him.

"A Man's Word Is His Bond" shares the virtue of being a "man of your word" and keeping promises, drawing examples from personal experiences with admirable figures like Bill Monroe and lamenting the lack of such integrity in modern society. It upholds the ideal of having one's actions match one's words as a matter of honor and character. This principle aligns with 1 John 2:4, which emphasizes the importance of keeping God's commandments as evidence of truly knowing and following Him. The scripture suggests that failing to uphold one's word and commitments is a form of dishonesty and hypocrisy, contradicting a genuine relationship with God. Thus, the message's advocacy for being trustworthy and following through on one's word reflects the biblical teaching that our actions should demonstrate integrity and align with our professed beliefs and values as followers of Christ.

Seeing Faith

1. How can following God's commandments be Christ-like?

_____

_____

_____

_____

_____

2. Is a person's oath bettered by swearing? What does the Bible teach about swearing?

_____

_____

_____

_____

_____

Seeing Faith

3. Over time oaths have evolved from (Ruth 4:7) plucking off a shoe and giving it to his neighbor, handshakes, filling out contracts signed by a notary, and recordings of an oral agreements. How do receipts protect a person's word?

_____

_____

_____

_____

_____

Pastor Carroll Allen
Ringgold Church of God in Ringgold, Georgia

Seeing Faith
What Is Honor?

How does one acquire it? Is honor a cloak that you can put on and take off at will?

I would say that honor is something that you acquire over time, much like putting on layers of clothes in the winter to stay warm. Once the layers are in place, you find yourself warm and comfortable.

Webster defines honor with a list of terms, including: respectful regard, esteem, worship, reputation, exalted rank, fame, magnanimity, scorn of meanness, self-respect, chastity, an outward mark of high esteem and glory.

Through the Congressional Medal of Honor, our country pays tribute to our soldiers who show valor in action against an enemy force.

There is a proverb, which says, "Ease and honor are seldom bedfellows."

I believe that there are many honorable people left in this world, although they are becoming harder to find.

Many people who cloak themselves in years of honor can at times find the weight of the layers a difficult load to bear. As the temperature rises, for some they begin to toss the layers aside to suit their personal needs and feelings.

It was poet Nicholas Boileau who said, "Honor is like an island, rugged and without a beach; once we have left it, we can never return."

I tend to agree — once you begin to throw off the layers, you are on the road to no longer being an honorable person. Unfortunately in life we find these people in every walk of life. It is difficult to tell at times when someone is

Seeing Faith

fully cloaked in honor or casting off his garments. Of course, there are many who simply never bothered to get dressed at all.

To describe those who truly have honor, I lean towards the words of former United States Air Force fighter pilot Scott O'Grady: "It wasn't the reward that mattered or the recognition you might harvest. It was your depth of commitment, your quality of service, the product of your devotion — these were the things that counted in a life. When you gave purely, the honor came in the giving, and that was honor enough."

Mark Twain said, "It is better to deserve honors and not have them than to have them and not deserve them."

It is sad in life when one does not receive the respect or recognition he or she has worked to receive, but one can find solace in the fact that if you remain layered in the fabric of honor, you are the better person for it.

Seeing Faith

John 12:26
If any man serve me, let him follow me; and where I am, there shall also my servant be: if any man serve me, him will my Father honor.

As a former Military Chaplain, I have served with many men and women that exemplify honor in the truest form. This honor did not fall into their laps or shine through in just one moment and one instance. These people lived a life of service and sacrifice. While we would all call these people heroes and while we all owe a debt to them for their service, it is another type of honor and another type of service that all of us can live towards. That is service to our Lord Jesus Christ. This verse in the Gospel of John tells us that to serve Jesus, we must follow Him. Following Jesus means that we must study and learn. We must engage personally with Him through the Holy Spirit. When we follow Him and experience Him, we can teach with authority...because we have been in his very presence! Following Jesus may lead us to sacrifice, difficulty and even laying down our own lives. The sacrifice is worth the reward! "...if any man may serve me, him will my Father honor".

Seeing Faith

1. Who do you see as a person of respect and honor? Who has been a positive influence in your Spiritual life?

_____

_____

_____

_____

_____

2. What traits and actions distinguish people of respect and honor?

_____

_____

_____

_____

_____

3. What does it mean to, "take up your cross and follow me"?

_____

_____

_____

_____

_____

Seeing Faith

4. How might you become a person that follows Christ, enters into his presence and receives honor from God the Father?

_____

_____

_____

_____

_____

Pastor Jamie Ellis
Woodstation Church in Ringgold, Georgia

Seeing Faith
Notes

Seeing Faith
The Energy Within One's Home

The golden chimes jingle as I walk through the porch door. "Hi Mom," I say, "I'm home." Of course, there is no one physically there to hear me. It is simply a greeting that I have grown accustomed to uttering for so many years I have yet to get over the mechanical habit. I imagine that in time uttering the words will simply fade as my mind gives in to the fact that I am doing something which could be perceived as silly if heard by another living human being.

I drop off the work I am carrying on the kitchen table, but in my head I hear her saying "Don't mess up the table." So, I pick it up and put it on the desk as I check the answering machine to find it blinking. I hit the machine, and it sends out a recorded message from a company wanting to sell me something. In a way, that little blinking light is comforting when there is a message from a friend, but when that light is still it sometimes brings a sigh.

I sit on the beige leather couch, kick off my black leather shoes, lean back and look around the living room. There is furniture from wall-to-wall, and each closet is filled, but there is an emptiness that just covers you. My niece Crystal was the first to comment on it when entering the house after my mother passed away. "The house feels different," she said.

"M*A*S*H" is playing on the television and I lose myself in the hilarity of the artistry of Alan Alda and company. For a while the emptiness is filled with a fictional world provided by those characters.

But soon reality must once again set in as I take on some mundane household chore such as sweeping the

Seeing Faith

hardwood floors or dusting the seemingly endless surfaces.

When someone has brought the vigor, the juice, the energy to a family's life and that person leaves, how does one carry on in the wake of their departure?

No matter how strong your faith, no matter how many cards or calls you receive, no matter how many times you find yourself with a lump in your throat and a tear in your eye, nothing can be done to ease the absence of that life's energy that is now missing from the house.

© 2005 Randall Franks Media

Pearl Franks and her son Randall attend the Georgia Music Hall of Fame Awards in 2005.

It is finally up to you to rebuild a new life's energy for your home, so when you walk in, you are not enveloped by the quiet emptiness. You must become the energy of the home, so when someone else walks in they find a feeling of warmth and welcome.

There must be a way to reach within oneself to make such a thing possible.

I struggled with that for quite a while, trying to infuse my own energy on our home while not taking away loving imprints of the shadows left on each and every item.

As I go through the process of picking up, cleaning up,

Seeing Faith

disposing of, moving about, I see improvements in the tidiness of the house but despite all my attempts, when I sit back down, pause, and look around, the house still feels empty. The warmth is gone.

I know that those of us that are Christians carry within us a special warmth given us by our faith in Jesus Christ and I know that as I do my daily tasks I work to allow that warmth to permeate what I do and shine out. I lean on Jesus to come with me wherever I go and I know God's angels are smoothing the way ahead of me and hopefully doing a bit of clean up in my wake.

Perhaps the warmth that God shares with me is not meant for me to transfer to a place like a house. Perhaps the warmth that each of us brings cannot be seen by us in our own reflection.

We cannot see our own warmth imprinted on a home. Only others can see that. So while I try to fill the emptiness for myself, in a way I am pouring the warmth into a bottomless pit that I will never fill. Only God can fill it in His time.

Isn't it wonderful that God's love is endless? No matter what I pour my inspired energies into, as long as this vessel of clay holds out, I can continue sharing His warmth with others and depend on Him to warm my heart, soul, mind and home with His love.

Seeing Faith

Notes

Seeing Faith

John 14:18
I will not leave you comfortless: I will come to you.

"The Energy Within One's Home" reflects on the feeling of emptiness and lack of warmth in one's home after the passing of a loved one who brought vibrancy and energy to the household. It expresses the struggle to infuse that same warmth and liveliness back into the home environment. This connects with the scripture John 14:18, where Jesus promises "I will not leave you comfortless; I will come to you."

1. Have you personally experienced the warmth of Christ's Presence?

_____

_____

_____

_____

_____

Seeing Faith

2. How have you dealt with the bereavement of losing someone close to you?

_____

_____

_____

_____

_____

3. Do you believe God is capable of comforting you in loss?

_____

_____

_____

_____

_____

Pastor Justin Gazaway
Catoosa Baptist Tabernacle in Ringgold, Georgia

Seeing Faith
Is It a God Thing?

Whenever I find myself facing an uncertain future, whether it's in work or my personal life, ultimately, I always find myself praying for Divine intervention.

I ask for guidance. I ask for forgiveness. I ask for patience. I ask for inspiration.

It always seems I am asking Him for something. But seldom am I thanking Him for what He has already given. From my personal experience, I know He hears and in His own way answers our requests. Sometimes the answer is no. We seldom understand that result. In fact, sometimes we interpret it, as He is not there. He is not listening. He has forsaken us.

From our own actions, many of us deserve to be forsaken but thankfully, as part of His family we will not be. We may not always get what our hearts desire. Our lives may not be easy. And sometimes they may be downright miserable. He is still with us.

In the face of what seems to be an ever-increasing presence of things that are ungodly being placed in front of us through media and in our own vision of the world around us,

I must conclude if there was ever a time for us to cry out to Him and ask His mercy upon us, it is now.

In recent weeks, I have been in prayer over lack of direction in my life, over falling short in His service and in trying to walk ever closer to Him. We all fall short of His love.

Yet, in the simplest thing, He can remind us "I am here,

Seeing Faith

and I love you."

I have a small golden key chain I was presented when I graduated from high school. I had never used it, only pulled it out and looked at it, thinking I will use it for a special occasion. Despite many years coming and going, I had not used it. I finally pulled it out and put my car keys on it. A small golden ball that served as a nut held the mechanism into place, thus holding the key ring into the golden circle into which it was mounted.

One day I went to the post office, I got out and the key ring fell apart dropping pieces to the ground. I bent over picked everything up and went on my way. I did not realize that the small golden ball that served a nut was not among what I picked up. I realized later at home it was gone. It could have unscrewed and fell off anywhere, I checked my clothes, the floorboard of the car, around the house, to no avail.

A couple a weeks passed when the thought hit me as I pulled into the post office again, go and look where you were parked that day. So, I did. I walked over to the empty parking space, took two steps beyond where my driver's door was and there it sat. It had rolled and sat there for two weeks with no vehicles rolling over it. Not a soul had noticed this little golden ball the size of a large bb. After I had become acclimated that I would never be able to use the key chain again. God sent a thought, moved my body, and there was something I had lost, a piece of something I cherished just lying on the ground safe in a place it should not have been.

I have spent a lifetime in the music industry. I have

Seeing Faith

strived to attain recognition for my music on the mainstream charts. That, along with awards is one of the ways we gauge our acceptance and success. I can tell you; those things do not just happen. Behind the scenes, there are many actions taken by you and folks who support you which facilitate such an opportunity. I have been praying tirelessly for career guidance for months. In February 2023, I was notified that I had topped the Cashbox Magazine music charts with a song I wrote with Cotton Carrier and released years ago — "God's Children" performed with the Watkins Family.

Never in my life had I been on the Cashbox charts, and then out of the blue I was number 1 on a mainstream entertainment chart with a song picked out of the blue by radio presenters with no behind the scenes promotion, no single release, not even trying. If that is not a God thing, I don't know what is.

Look for the God things in your life. They are there, big and small. And when you find them, don't forget to thank Him!

Seeing Faith

Psalm 103:1-5
Bless the LORD, O my soul: And all that is within me, bless his holy name.
Bless the LORD, O my soul, And forget not all his benefits:
Who forgiveth all thine iniquities; Who healeth all thy diseases;
Who redeemeth thy life from destruction; Who crowneth thee with lovingkindness and tender mercies;
Who satisfieth thy mouth with good things; So that thy youth is renewed like the eagle's.

Sometimes we forget that faith is faith. We are believing in something that hasn't been fully seen (and sometimes might not be until after our death). Yes, of course, we can read the words of Psalm 103 and imagine many scenarios worthy of joyous praise but we should also read it and sing it when the future is uncertain. Sometimes, in the end all we can do is bless the Lord, give God praise and trust God with the results; and sometimes those results end up being better than we ever imagined.

Seeing Faith

1. How does the act of remembering and acknowledging God's benefits contribute to our spiritual well-being and gratitude?

_____

_____

_____

_____

_____

2. In what ways have you experienced Gods redemption from difficult circumstances or moments of despair?

_____

_____

_____

_____

_____

Seeing Faith

3. How does God satisfy us with good and renew our strength, and how can we rely on this promise in times of need?

_____

_____

_____

_____

_____

Pastor Chris Bryant
Ringgold United Methodist Church in Ringgold, Georgia

Seeing Faith
The Seeds of Wisdom Spit Forth

As I sat on the back porch watching the grass die, I could not help but find myself in my mind's eye sitting similarly on my grandmother's porch. It was a summer where I spent a lot of time with my Grandma Kitty and Aunt Norma Jean. Flossie, the milk cow, was meandering through the yard headed for a shade tree where she laid down and tried to create a bit of a breeze using her tail.

Kitty

Grandma was doing a much better job in her rocker with her funeral home fan and her right arm. In fact, she managed to move enough that I picked up a bit of the breeze as mother and I went back and forth on the porch swing. Norma Jean leaned back in a ladderback chair against the wall in a way that was abnormally still for her.

It was one of those days once referred to as the dog days of summer. I never quite understood except perhaps that we all sat around with our tongues hanging out of our mouths panting, or so it seemed to me as a kid.

Norma Jean

After a while, I just couldn't stand being still so I headed down to the branch to dangle my feet in the water. You know that works a lot better if you take off your shoes and socks. I never said I was real bright back then, or maybe it was just the heat.

Before I knew what had happened, I looked around and everyone from the porch had joined me, and you know

Seeing Faith

there were smiles on their faces. They actually remembered to take their shoes off.

It was like the branch filled our bodies with a sense of hope, hope that the heat would pass, and we would once again feel like ourselves again.

It wasn't long though until I realized it wasn't me that had drawn the group to the branch, especially when I noticed mother had spread out a red and white tablecloth on the bank beneath a tree. On it was a large knife and a cutting board and a saltshaker, but there was nothing else.

What I did not know was that Grandma had a surprise for me. She sent me down into the deepest spot in the branch and told me to reach in for a surprise.

There was a deep green watermelon from the garden that was now cold as can be from the water running over it for most of the day.

I lifted it out and brought it up and set it on the cutting board. My shoes squished with each step.

We all now gathered around as mother cut the watermelon in pieces and we each began eating our fill.

Red fruit with a touch of salt and all those black seeds. How do you be polite with all those black seeds?

I followed Grandma's lead and realized she was throwing the conventions of proper etiquette out the window. Rather than disposing of them quietly in a napkin, she suggested that we have a contest and see how far we all could reach spitting a seed.

We all took turns, seeing who could get across the branch. It is amazing how far the ladies could spit. They made it to the other side almost every time. Occasionally

Seeing Faith

one fell short and down the branch it floated.

With each round, we found more laughter, each of us eventually won, and by the time we finished the melon, we had almost forgotten how hot it was when we started.

Our heat-induced melancholy was lost to the mischief of a melon and all its little seeds.

As an added bonus, next year, the watermelons were so close to the branch, they didn't even have to be carried and put in, they just rolled in themselves.

Seeing Faith

Psalm 23:3
He restoreth my soul: he leadeth me in the paths of righteousness for his name's sake.

Isaiah 40:31
But they that wait upon the LORD shall renew their strength; they shall mount up with wings as eagles; they shall run, and not be weary; and they shall walk, and not faint.

Isaiah 58:11
And the LORD shall guide thee continually, and satisfy thy soul in drought, and make fat thy bones: and thou shalt be like a watered garden, and like a spring of water, whose waters fail not.

Lamentations 3:21-24
This I recall to my mind, therefore have I hope. It is of the LORD'S mercies that we are not consumed, because his compassions fail not. They are new every morning: great is thy faithfulness. The LORD is my portion, saith my soul; therefore will I hope in him.

Seeing Faith

There are moments when our surroundings seem to mirror a parched and desolate wasteland. The trials and tribulations of life can intensify like the relentless scorching sun, producing a string of anxieties that threaten to overwhelm us. Yet, amid this arid terrain exists a solution of unparalleled strength — the antidote to our distress is none other than the wellspring of hope and, more particularly, hope in Christ. Christian hope is not a mere whimsical longing but an unwavering, confident trust in God. The Apostle Peter said: "Repent ye therefore, and be converted, that your sins may be blotted out, when the times of refreshing shall come from the presence of the Lord" (Acts 3:19).

The "time of refreshing" carries the idea of spiritual renewal that produces spiritual blessings. This divine moment encompasses far more than a mere physical sensation; it embodies the essence of spiritual rejuvenation. God gives us something even better than water. He gives us a fresh start and hope through His endless kindness. It is like picking the sweetest fruit from His never-ending garden of grace. God will not fill your mouth with watermelon seeds, but He will fill your mouth with praise as you delight in Him. You will find solace and joy as you turn your hearts towards Him. Psalm 71:8 should be your heart's desire: "Let my mouth be filled with thy praise and with thy honour all the day."

Seeing Faith

1. The message describes a heartwarming scene of simple pleasures, such as eating watermelon and spitting seeds that brought joy and refreshment during a hot summer day. How does this relate to the biblical principle found in Psalm 23:3, where God promises to "restore our souls" and lead us in paths of righteousness?

_____

_____

_____

_____

_____

2. The commentary highlights the idea of finding hope and spiritual refreshment in the presence of the Lord, even in the midst of life's trials and difficulties, as described in Acts 3:19. How can we cultivate this kind of unwavering hope and trust in God's provision, as exemplified in the scriptures from Isaiah and Lamentations?

_____

_____

_____

_____

_____

Seeing Faith

3. In Lamentations 3:21-24, the writer declares that the Lord's mercies are new every morning, and that His faithfulness is a source of hope. How can meditating on God's compassion and steadfast love help us to find joy and refreshment, even in the most challenging or "drought-like" seasons of life?

_____

_____

_____

_____

_____

Dr. David Sampson
Parkway Baptist in Fort Oglethorpe, Georgia

Seeing Faith
Notes

Seeing Faith
Some Flour, a Broom and a Lesson on Being Needed

As I look down at the flour on the floor and the straw of the broom as it meets the floor at the edge of heap, I swiftly move it through the white powder. In the motion, my mind sweeps over my memories and I find myself standing beside the table in my boyhood home. My Grandma Kitty is standing at the end of the broom sweeping flour that I had managed to spill as we were preparing biscuits and getting ready to bake a batch of cookies.

"We don't have to mention this to anyone," she said. "This will be our little secret."

She moves the flour into the dustpan and she taps it on the edge of the trashcan.

"Where were we?" she said. "Yes, we need some lard to add to the flour."

"Will Crisco do?" I asked.

"Sure," she said.

I grabbed it from the cupboard beneath the phone behind the kitchen door and sat it on the table next to her.

So with her hands she worked up the biscuit dough and patted out the biscuits placing them on the baking sheet.

"Now, that's done and we can concentrate on the cookies for this afternoon," she said.

Mother was hosting the neighborhood ladies and some friends for tea.

Grandma Kitty was making the only visit she ever made to our home. She had been sick dealing with a heart problem and had left the mountains to convalesce at our home.

Seeing Faith

Despite the fact, she had never lived in the city, she was thriving and enjoying the opportunity to participate in all the activities that kept our home hopping when I was a boy and my parents were in full swing with their work and volunteering in the community.

She found some new friends with our elderly neighbors and in just a short time, she and my Aunt Norma Jean were changing their routines that once centered on the farm, the chickens, the cows, and the garden, to do anything they wanted in the city.

After quite a while of rest, she still found comfort in being able to do. I think no matter what afflicts us, how old we are, or what challenges we face, we need the ability to give and feel useful in our talents.

Grandma Kitty had run a farmhouse from her mid teens to her mid seventies. She could do it in her sleep, and though she had slowed, she still wanted to contribute even though she was in her daughter's home.

Kitty

Aunt Norma Jean was developmentally challenged from childhood and never lived outside of home while my grandparents were living. Though she faced many challenges, she was able to learn many functional tasks of working around the farm and numerous games that the children enjoyed playing along with her. During the visit to our home, she joined right in around the house helping to take some of the

Seeing Faith

worries of day-to-day cleaning off mom and helping with anything needed for Grandma. She was excited like I was in the new activities we chose to fill the days and meeting new people who rotated in and out of our lives on a daily basis.

As Grandma Kitty improved, she took the reins of a few activities in the kitchen, which brought her to this adventure in my memory. Between the mixing and the spilling flour, I found my Grandma in a way I had not before. I found a smile that was seldom seen in the stoic face of the Appalachian woman I knew. The burdens of the farm lifted off her back. Her domain, rather than endless acres, was simply a 12 by 12 foot kitchen.

I don't remember how long she stayed with us. Somewhere around a month, as best I recall, but eventually our time together would end and she would return to the farm. Though there were discussions of them coming to live with us permanently, the input of mother's other siblings prevailed and that would not happen.

The day she left was a sad day for me: I loved having her and Norma Jean with us, and as I look back, I think they both thrived and seemed so happy. While I learned so much in my times with them on the farm, I will never forget these moments of sharing our lives with them when as we baked my grandmother taught me how important it is to feel you contribute to the world each and every day.

Have you made your contribution today? Have your helped someone in your life feel useful and needed? Don't miss a chance to uplift the life of someone you love!

Seeing Faith
Notes

Seeing Faith

Psalms 71:17
O God, thou hast taught me from my youth: and hitherto have I declared thy wondrous works.

Psalms 71:18
Now also when I am old and grayheaded, O God, forsake me not; until I have shewed thy strength unto this generation, and thy power to every one that is to come.

"Some Flour, a Broom and a Lesson on Being Needed" recounts a cherished memory of the writer's grandmother, Kitty, staying with their family and finding joy in simple acts like baking together in the kitchen. Despite her age and health challenges, Kitty gained a renewed sense of purpose and usefulness through these small contributions. This experience taught the writer the importance of helping loved ones feel needed and able to share their talents. This aligns with the scriptures in Psalms 71:17-18, where the Psalmist declares his intention to proclaim God's wondrous works from his youth until old age, asking the Lord not to forsake him so he can display God's strength to every generation.

Seeing Faith

1. Do you believe you were created by God on purpose with a purpose?

_____

_____

_____

_____

_____

2. If you are a Christian have you understood your purpose in Christ?

_____

_____

_____

_____

_____

3. If you are a Christian will you purpose to live your life for God's glory from this day until your last? If your still alive He is not done with you!

_____

_____

_____

_____

_____

Pastor Justin Gazaway
Catoosa Baptist Tabernacle in Ringgold, Georgia

Seeing Faith

The Rhythm of the Waves

The waves beat rhythmically against the shore in what seemed an endless pattern.

I had stretched out in the back of my white Ford station-wagon near the shore, and the sound lulled me quickly to sleep.

As I woke up, I walked slowly along the beach and watched the sun rise up over the horizon and cast rays of yellow and orange across the water.

The wet sand pushed up between my toes as I picked up shells and tossed them back into the sea from whence they came. The scent of salt water was in the air. I breathed deeply.

As an adult, I can return to those feelings I had in my youth. One deep breath of that salt water air, and I am transported back to a time when my future seemed filled with all the potential of any dream in my heart or mind.

My opportunities were as boundless as the sands that stretched along the beach and all I needed to do was pursue them.

I did pursue so many of them — music, acting, writing, and directing.

As I stood on the shore more recently, I never expected to find the sense of endless possibilities again. So many of those ideals we cast away with the passing of time in our lives or as we make choices.

But almost like finding a breath of fresh air, the beauty of what filled my senses invigorated my hopes and dreams once again that what God gifts within my soul is possible.

Seeing Faith

In my heart, I heard in the rhythm of the waves, I can do all things through Christ who strengthens me.

So this time as I shook the sand off my shoes, I knew once again that the path was even more clear and possible.

I hope you find your path in the dreams that God places in your heart.

Seeing Faith

Ecclesiates 12:1
Remember now thy Creator in the days of thy youth, while the evil days come not, nor the years draw nigh, when thou shalt say, I have no pleasure in them;

James 4:14
Whereas ye know not what shall be on the morrow. For what is your life? It is even a vapour, that appeareth for a little time, and then vanisheth away.

Everyone has what I like to call, "A memory time capsule". There are certain scents, songs, people, places that tend to bring faded memories rushing back to the forefront of our minds. Some are good memories while others may not be so pleasant. See Matthew 6:19-20. God wants us to create eternal memories with Him. Too many times we focus on the temporal when we should be focusing on the eternal (2 Corinthians 4:18). When you get near the end of life and return to your ocean shore as Randall did, what will your memories be? I am reminded of that old C. T. Studd song which states, "Only one life, 'twill soon be past, only what's done for Christ will last." Will you do something for Christ today?

Seeing Faith

1. What are some of your fondest memories?

_____

_____

_____

_____

_____

2. How many of these memories would you say are temporal and how many of them would you categorize as eternal?

_____

_____

_____

_____

_____

3. At the end of your life, what would you classify as your greatest achievement? Does that achievement include God?

_____

_____

_____

_____

_____

Pastor Jeff Brown
Valley View Baptist Church in Flintstone, Georgia

Seeing Faith

Don't Watch the World Go By: Use Your Imagination

The water swished over the rocks below and created a gurgling sound as I sat dangling my feet off the bridge. I was just high enough above the water where if I could stretch out as far as I could I still couldn't touch it. I dreamed of the day when I would be big enough to do so.

As I sat there, I counted the leaves that floated beneath the bridge and imagined that each one was a ship heading out to an adventure at sea.

It was early enough in the fall that the whole fleet wasn't setting sail beneath me.

There was so much imagination that filled my childhood. I would move from one imagined adventure to another, filling my days with sword fights, gun battles, cavalry charges, and Indian skirmishes. If I had managed to gather a few comrades in arms, we might manage building a fort, stocking it with pinecones, and then take turns setting off with a huge offensive to capture it.

When I tired of war games, I would move on to building things, damming up creeks like a beaver, digging holes that were big enough for a root cellar, gathering up fallen logs to build a cabin façade, pretending that I was on the frontier.

I was blessed to be able to be a kid, play like one and have the environment where my imagination could run and I was allowed to explore and experience what I held within my head.

Today, I see so many youths who are tied mentally to a

Seeing Faith

chair with their imagination being dictated to them by whatever game is coming across their television, their computer or their phone. I am sure they find the adventures just as stimulating as I did, but their adventures are created by the imagination of game designers, and they are simply taking trips in someone else's imagination.

They sit there idle as they ask to be fed by someone else's imaginative situational adventure.

Same is true of the adults who await that next movie, TV show, or sporting event to take them away for a period of time, rather than creating something themselves.

I really think God provided us a mind so that we will use it to create, entertain, invent, and find ways to make life more amazing.

So much time and energy is lost in pursuits that probably do not inspire others but simply feed an appetite for diversion — that is, "entertain me." Our mind wishes to be filled by others, rather than doing it ourselves.

I applaud those of you who use your time and energies to create, engage, encourage and change the world around you.

If you have not tried it in a while, there is no better time than the present. Pick up your pen, start writing that story you always wanted to write; what about that thing you always wanted to build? Give it a try. Nothing ventured, nothing gained.

Seeing Faith

Romans 12:2
And be not conformed to this world: but be ye transformed by the renewing of your mind, that ye may prove what is that good, and acceptable, and perfect, will of God.

Philippians 4:8
Finally, brethren, whatsoever things are true, whatsoever things are honest, whatsoever things are just, whatsoever things are pure, whatsoever things are lovely, whatsoever things are of good report; if there be any virtue, and if there be any praise, think on these things.

Today most children, as well as adults, are inundated and overrun with empty things that compete for and thereafter consume our time, attention, energy, mental capacity and, ultimately, our affections. From smartphones to TV and film, from social media to video games, the outpouring of the trappings of this world seek to keep us overly busy, overstimulated, and preoccupied to the point that our minds are not fixed on the Lord and our hearts are far from Him. While a born again believer is in fact "in the world," he or

Seeing Faith

she is not "of the world." The Lord does not intend for the mind of the believer to be lulled, dulled, or diverted away from Him. The born again believer is to be a transformed soul, not a conformed one. The Bible tells us that we are transformed not by dulling our minds, but my renewing our minds.

1. How might a Christian guard and renew his or her mind?

_____

_____

_____

_____

_____

2. Examine 2 Corinthians 4:16. With what frequency should renewal occur?

_____

_____

_____

_____

_____

Seeing Faith

3. Read 1 Corinthians 3:12-13. What are some things in your life today that will show up as gold, silver, and precious stones one day?

_____

_____

_____

_____

_____

Assistant Pastor Mike Smith
Valley View Baptist Church in Flintstone, Georgia

Seeing Faith
Notes

Seeing Faith
A Leaf of Strength

The leaf hung tightly to a lonely limb and swayed in the air. It seemed, to say to the world, "I am not done, and you are not going to make me fall down no matter what you throw at me." All of its fellow leaves had given up the ghost and blown in whatever direction the wind desired them to go. Some managed to find a resting place at the foot of the majestic oak tree to spend the winter and become the woodland blanket upon which the rain would fall before soaking into the ground.

My Grandad sat quietly on the porch and stared at the leaf bobbing in the wind.

He had come back from a powerful stroke that took the wind from his earthly sails. Before, it had seemed that he would bend to nothing. Now, he could barely lift himself from his chair.

On this fall day, spying that lone leaf seemed to fortify him more than anything that anyone could say to bolster his spirits. He stared endlessly and watched its fight, and as the fight struggled on from one day to two, to a week, his personal strength seemed to grow.

He managed each day. No matter how the wind blew or what elements forced themselves past the mountain homestead, he walked out to the porch to spend some time sitting, later leaning against the porch post, and then standing as upright as the years would allow. He was always looking off towards the oak tree and its one holdout to the whims of the world and said nothing that revealed the focus of his internal thoughts.

Seeing Faith

As the winter came on strong, he would rise up and with his cane in hand, he eventually walked off the porch and towards that mighty oak tree going as far as he felt comfortable then returning to the porch. With each trip he got closer to his goal and he soon reached the tree and looked straight up towards the hanging leaf.

There were a few times he would take one hand, lean against the trunk of the tree and with the other lift his cane as far as he could and try to hit the leaf that centered his focus. He was just shy of reaching it, and he would eventually tire and return to the warmth of the fireplace inside.

The light covering of snow did not even dissuade him from making his trek to the oak and returning home. With each passing day he grew stronger.

Kitty and Bill Bruce sit on the porch of their house below the Gravelly Spur.

By the first signs of spring, he no longer limited his walking to just the tree. He began taking on more of the activities that made his day sing around the farm.

One spring day, the tree had refilled all its limbs and the greenery made it full and majestic. Grandad could no longer see the lone leaf from the porch, so he decided to make another trek to see what had become of his now old companion who he fought alongside against the world's

Seeing Faith

elements.

As he reached the tree, he looked on the ground to find it to no avail. So he turned his gaze upward. Amongst the lush green leaves, there it was — one brown leaf still holding on to its place amidst the green youngsters around it.

Grandad's face seemed to change as he fought back the effects of the stroke moved to show a smile.

He raised his cane, almost in a sense of a salute to the lone leaf, then turned and walked down the trail. Emboldened by the lone leaf, he was figuring to hold on to his place in the world and stand as the man he was inside, no matter what nature threw against him.

We need more people in this world who work to overcome what they face and find the inner strength that God placed within each of His creations.

Seeing Faith
Notes

Seeing Faith

Hebrews 10:23
Let us hold fast the profession of our faith without wavering; (for he is faithful that promised;)

1 Corinthians 15:58
Therefore, my beloved brethren, be ye stedfast, unmoveable, always abounding in the work of the Lord, forasmuch as ye know that your labour is not in vain in the Lord.

This Christian walk we're on can feel challenging at times. Our Bible even tells us that if you set out to live Godly, you will face persecution in some manner or another. At times today, the narrow way we're walking can feel like being on an island, all alone. Secular society tries its best to make you feel like you're a solitary, sole brown leaf, clinging to the truth, all by your lonesome. You're holding on tight while the world seeks to blow you around with every wind of doctrine, trying to rattle you, trying to shake you loose, trying to sift you! But, beloved, our Lord implores us to be steadfast and unmoveable. Cling to the truth and refuse to let go, even if you're the only one left in the dead of winter. Our effort, our labour is not in vain in

Seeing Faith

the Lord. There is a time of refreshing right around the corner. Hold fast!

1. What are some ways in which you're clinging to the truth in the face of strong opposition?

_____

_____

_____

_____

_____

2. How might you help when you see a brother or sister barely hanging on?

_____

_____

_____

_____

_____

Seeing Faith

3. How does knowing of the Lord Jesus' unspotted, unmarred, and perfect faithfulness embolden you to "hold fast" in your life?

_____

_____

_____

_____

_____

Assistant Pastor Mike Smith
Valley View Baptist Church in Flintstone, Georgia

Seeing Faith
Notes

Seeing Faith
Dreams that Inspire

I ran down the dark corridor. My heart was beating fast as I heard footsteps rushing towards me from behind. I opened the door at the end as it swung inward and next, I found myself dangling from the doorknob over a dark pit that seemed bottomless.

I held on for dear life trying to pull myself back up into the hall.

Which was worse? Falling into the dark unknown or making it back to the solid hallway where I was being chased by who knows what.

Thankfully, I didn't have to find out as my alarm went off bringing me safely back into my bedroom.

Dreaming can sometimes bring us to smiles, sometimes to fear, sometimes in between.

I have spent time in many dreams sitting and talking with loved ones who were long passed. Those moments are usually cherished opportunities to spend a few more minutes with a dear friend or relative.

Other dreams have found me in places I have never been experiencing new adventures with people I have never known or with faces I recognize. Those are usually quite comforting as well.

As a youth I saw dreams as roadmaps to where God wanted to take me, and often he placed the footsteps out ahead of me as if they were flashing in neon. Those took me places I could have never dreamed of in my waking hours.

Are dreams simply our imagination running wild?

Seeing Faith

Are messages from our past, our future, or from our loved ones gone on hidden within?

I know that people in various forms of study have spent endless hours trying to answer those types of questions. From the Biblical stories of Joseph interpreting the dreams of pharaoh, to whatever scenario one might surmise from their own research, dreams play a vital part in our lives. They give us relief, sometimes hope, and sometimes fear. No matter what they provide, if you are blessed with a good dream experience, be thankful for what has passed. Perhaps it is a God wink to uplift.

If it's not such a good experience, maybe that is an inducement to examine your life and find where you might improve to clear your heart and mind, so next time it can be.

For me, despite a few frightening ones along the way, the good ones outweigh those, and from time to time, I do believe God's drops in a bit of guidance here and there to make my life better, if I only recall it.

So, get a good night's rest...

Seeing Faith

Daniel 2:1-3
And in the second year of the reign of Nebuchadnezzar Nebuchadnezzar dreamed dreams, wherewith his spirit was troubled, and his sleep brake from him..
Then the king commanded to call the magicians, and the astrologers, and the sorcerers, and the Chaldeans, for to shew the king his dreams. So they came and stood before the king.
And the king said unto them, I have dreamed a dream, and my spirit was troubled to know the dream.

A good counselor will tell you that sometimes a dream we have, especially those that seem to disturb us, lets our conscious know that our subconscious is still troubled or working through something. Yes, perhaps a dream we have, especially the more wild and ridiculous ones are nothing more than the result of our eating too late the evening prior. But there are other dreams that hit home, touch on a piece of reality perhaps with a twist and we're left wondering about it. Is it God? If so, what is that a about, a warning, a clarity, a direction …or maybe a blessing?

Seeing Faith

1. Have you ever experienced a longing for clarity or insight into a situation?

_____

_____

_____

_____

_____

2. What lessons can we learn about the limitations of seeking answers from worldly sources rather than relying on God's wisdom and guidance?

_____

_____

_____

_____

_____

3. How can we cultivate a deeper trust in God's sovereignty and providence, even in moments of uncertainty and anxiety?

_____

_____

_____

_____

_____

Pastor Chris Bryant
Ringgold United Methodist Church in Ringgold, Georgia

Seeing Faith
The Creeping Doldrums

Do you ever find yourself enjoying a perfectly good day and then before your know what has happened you find yourself in the midst of a spell of listlessness or despondency?

Those energetic goals that were there when you woke up have slipped back down deep under the covers. So you decide to go looking for them only to find yourself shackled to the bedpost and unable to pull yourself back out of the bed.

What about the times you are simply sitting at your desk and there are so many tasks before you, but you just seemed baffled at what to do next?

Well my friend, you are suffering from the creeping doldrums. They just come up from out of nowhere, spawned sometimes by a thought, a piece of music, the sound of the rain on the roof, or some aspect of your life which seems to pull you down into the mud and keep you stuck.

When I was a boy, we use to go spelunking a lot, and I remember one cave we called the peanut butter cave. As you walked through, you were most likely to lose a shoe before getting out. You would fight with all your might to get through it, and it would take a lot of your energy. I don't remember one of my fellow cavers that ever were left there stuck in the mud.

No matter how productive and positive one's life may seem, we all have days where the creeping doldrums invade our well-being.

What is the solution?

Seeing Faith

For me, I find I just have to get up out of bed and trudge forward through the peanut butter cave until I have reached the opening that leads me back into the Light.

Simple tasks will fill the day until our mind and body are ready to once again tackle the big goals.

Now, by my excursion down this road, I am not saying a person does not need some down time to rest and restore. It's just when we let the creeping doldrums steal from us even the enjoyment of rest that a real problem ensues.

Rest in the reading of a good book. Rest in watching your favorite TV show or film. Rest in talking with friends gathered to watch a sporting event. All of these help us to recharge.

The key to the rest is not to let the creeping doldrums convince us we need even more than we do and before we know it our unoccupied mind is filling itself with negative thoughts.

So, if you find yourself with the creeping doldrums, get out your old shoes and trudge on through the mud until you get to the other side. You will be stronger and next time it will be easier to leave the creeping doldrums behind.

Seeing Faith

Philippians 4:8
Finally, brethren, whatsoever things are true, whatsoever things are honest, whatsoever things are just, whatsoever things are pure, whatsoever things are lovely, whatsoever things are of good report; if there be any virtue, and if there be any praise, think on these things.

"The Creeping Doldrums" encourages us to overcome despondency by using simple tasks and activities while trudging through the "peanut butter cave" heading towards the light allows each of us to redirect our thoughts towards virtuous and uplifting matters. As mentioned in the scripture filling one's mind with wholesome and edifying pursuits is a valuable use of effort.

The message reflects this scriptural exhortation by advocating for a proactive mindset and approach to combat feelings of despondency or lack of motivation. Just as the verse instructs believers to dwell on thoughts that are true, honest, just, pure, lovely, and praiseworthy, the message encourages pushing through "the creeping doldrums" by engaging in simple tasks and activities that can recharge and refocus the mind on positive pursuits. The metaphor of

Seeing Faith

trudging through the metaphorical "peanut butter cave" until reaching the light aligns with the principle of intentionally redirecting one's thoughts toward virtuous and uplifting matters. By emphasizing the importance of not allowing negative thought patterns to take root during rest periods, the message underscores the need for disciplining one's mind, akin to the scriptural directive. Additionally, the suggestions of reading, watching enjoyable shows, or spending time with friends mirror the spirit of Philippians 4:8 by advocating for filling one's mind with wholesome and edifying pursuits that can overcome despondency.

1. What specific activities, hobbies, or practices help you dwell on the positive thoughts and virtues encouraged in Philippians 4:8 when you find yourself struggling with "the creeping doldrums"?

_____

_____

_____

_____

_____

Seeing Faith

2. How can we cultivate a mindset that is vigilant against allowing negative or despondent thought patterns to take root, as warned against in the message?

_____

_____

_____

_____

_____

3. Beyond personal applications, how can we encourage and support others who may be experiencing periods of listlessness or despondency, pointing them towards the uplifting truths found in Philippians 4:8?

_____

_____

_____

_____

_____

Seeing Faith

Notes

Seeing Faith
Living in the Right Path

Knowing one's best direction in life can be an ever-changing debate within your own head.

As someone who has spent a life in entertainment, I often look at my situation to weigh my perception of what I do with the reality of the logistics of life.

I find myself fretting over some aspect of where my road has taken me and wonder whether I veered from the appointed path set out for me.

Was I meant to do something different in life? Did I choose what God intended?

Those are questions that I am sure many people ponder, especially as the children are screaming at each other in the back seat of the car, the bills on the table appear to be much higher that any hope of payment, or the honey do list becomes a small paperback.

I learned many years ago from actor Carroll O'Connor in a deep conversation about the human condition and differences in people that in life we often spend our time listening to the problems of others as he or she seeks empathy.

He told me in that shared experience there is a sense of uplifting that the sharer can gain if received and responded to properly, while the listener can overt a draining of spirit while sharing comfort.

"Everyone has the same problems," he told me. "Different folks just have a different number of zeros attached to them."

So in some way, that list of things people endure mentioned above along with a long list of others is not unique

Seeing Faith

Randall Franks (right) and Carroll O'Connor pause on the set of "In the Heat of the Night."

to us. We all have moments of doubt when we wonder if we are on the right path. Shouldn't life be easier if we were? Not necessarily.

We can be within the path set forth by God before we were a twinkle in our father's eye in His purpose for us to fulfill His mission, and life could be very difficult.

If we have accepted Christ into our life, then we are in His light. We may choose to put on a blindfold at times as we make a choice outside our appropriate path, but He is always with us shining His light waiting for us to reflect what He is sharing.

When I begin to sink into the questions of my choices, my circumstances, my feelings, I then remember that ultimately, I am striving in His will and if He wishes me to be in a different situation, He will open the doors and reveal the path.

I just need to remain ready, prepared, and always be working to improve the opportunities within my life, career and my relationships with family and friends.

Carroll's "Archie" character might have told me to "stifle" as I began whining about my life and after a few lines

Seeing Faith

proceeded with "You meathead, you...."

Sometimes we need to say that to ourselves, "You meathead, you!" Life is a blessing, even in the worst situation you can experience; there are others who have greater need in the world. So as "Archie" could have shared: "Be like that real American John Wayne, and pick yourselves up by your boot straps there, and just get on with it. Do what is right and God will look after you."

Seeing Faith

Notes

Seeing Faith

Psalm 55:22
Cast thy burden upon the Lord, and he shall sustain thee: he shall never suffer the righteous to be moved.

We are very fortunate that God's plan for our salvation does not depend on our ability to earn it or to deserve it, or for us to perfect by our own ability! God's plan for our salvation, and ultimately, that is His plan for us, depends on His Grace, through His son Jesus. God has given each of us specific gifts, talents, interests, skills and abilities, and also a call to use those for advancing the Gospel into the world. He never promised us that it would be easy! He never promised us that we wouldn't face opposition to difficulties. What he has promised us, is that he will never forsake us or abandon us! He walks with us and walks before us, and he gives wisdom, guidance and comfort. In this verse of Psalm, He reminds us that we can cast our burden on Him and will give us comfort. Furthermore, he promises that not only will we be comforted, that He will help us to hold our ground...in fact, he states that through Him...we will not be moved! Our day to day lives may be hard and full of pain and loss, but when we cast our eyes to the eternal, and we participate in the work of the Gospel, we will be comforted, uplifted and anchored in place by the love

Seeing Faith

and grace of our Father and our Savior!

1. How did you first hear the Gospel, and what made you respond to the call of salvation?

_____

_____

_____

_____

_____

2. What are some unique gifts, talents and abilities that you have that God can use for His Gospel ministry?

_____

_____

_____

_____

_____

Seeing Faith

3. Have you ever shared your faith with another person? How did that go?

_____

_____

_____

_____

_____

4. Knowing that God's ultimate plan for all of us is to be saved by grace, and then to bring others into that same relationship, what things will you do to share the Gospel with others?

_____

_____

_____

_____

_____

Pastor Jamie Ellis
Woodstation Church in Ringgold, Georgia

Seeing Faith
Notes

Seeing Faith

Assure People We Place Our Faith in Are Real

The airwaves each election season are filled with those tauting that they are the best choice to lead our country, states, counties and cities.

I was honored to serve in my hometown as a city council member for 12.5 years, so I am speaking not only as someone who is on the outside but in some respects someone who was on the inside.

When a candidate says something, is it what they believe, or is it what they want us to hear?

That is a question each of us should ask when we finally find someone we feel could fill a spot of authority as our representative and leader.

I have seen firsthand how some candidates and/or elected officials seek to simply say what it takes to get elected and then do what they want rather than reflect what they said.

If there is a previous record to review, take the time to see the types of things that the person has supported, said, or voted for in the past.

What have they done consistently?

This information should provide a good road map of their plans for the future to see if they align with what they are saying publicly now.

Now a person can change what he or she believes through garnering more or new information, so it is possible that in this respect a leopard can change its spots.

One can only hope that the impact on the candidate's

Seeing Faith

thinking is true and not just politically prudent to gain the support of voters or other powerful political allies.

Sadly, that does occur and those are the types of candidates that should be ferreted out and returned to their daily tasks at home rather than serving in any office.

Ultimately, any candidate who wets his finger and holds it up to see which way political winds are blowing will in the end be a person who is seeking office simply to hold office and wield the power, privilege or influence that affords.

These types of individuals who manage to smile past the voters into an office are great ammunition for those who argue for term limits.

At this time what we need greatest are voters who spend the time to learn about the candidates before going to cast a vote.

An educated registered voter is the greatest potential tool that our forefathers hoped would keep this unique experiment of the United States alive. Without each of us stepping up and fulfilling our part of that experiment, it is sure that one day in our future, we will be bowing to someone who is not elected and accepting laws and customs which none of us ever thought we would see in the American land of red, white and blue.

Pray for the candidates so they may be worthy of election; pray for the voters so they may be informed; pray for our country so that our freedom and our nation may endure.

Seeing Faith

Romans 13:1-3
Let every soul be subject unto the higher powers. For there is no power but of God: the powers that be are ordained of God.
Whosoever therefore resisteth
the power, resisteth the ordinance of God: and they that resist shall receive to themselves damnation.
For rulers are not a terror to good works, but to the evil. Wilt thou then not be afraid of the power? do that which is good, and thou shalt have praise of the same.

The apostle Paul, in the Book of Romans tells us that there is no power, authority or government in place that God has not ordained or empowered. That is sometimes a hard to believe or at least hard to accept reality! We have to remember that God doesn't think or act or rule in the same way that we would. If I were in charge, I would install a government that made the path to prosperity straight and achievable for anyone that would work for it. I would install a government that allowed individual freedoms and encouraged people to work together and respect one another's rights. In other words, maybe an idealized version of

Seeing Faith

the Representative Republic that we have in the United States. That certainly isn't the government that is most prevalent throughout the world, and seems difficult to protect and hold onto here in the U.S.A.

Romans tells us that no government has any authority except what he ordains. God has a different economy than we have. God wants nothing more than for each of us to come into a life changing, soul saving relationship with Him. Some may be drawn to Him through ease of life and freedom, others may be drawn to him through struggle and difficulty.

In our system, things are very different than in the time that this text was written. We are called to respect the authority in place, but we are also called, by our country to be involved in the process to select our leaders. We have a voice in who those leaders are, and have an opportunity to act, on God's behalf at the ballot box! Christians, filled with the Holy Spirit, are agents of God. We must educate ourselves, both in what God would have us do, and then on what the candidates proclaim as their platform, then we must choose the candidate that will most closely represent the views that God would ordain. Voting is not only a freedom of our country, it is a call to do God's work and will in our world!

Seeing Faith

1. Paul tells us in Romans that we must respect the authority that is in place, and goes so far as to say that it is ordained by God! Are there examples from History that help make this point, or examples that make it difficult to accept this point?

_____

_____

_____

_____

_____

2. Voting numbers are usually very low and disappointing! This often makes us wonder if the true will of the people is truly being done. Church attendance, is also very low compared to the number of people in the population. How can we share our faith more effectively, while also educating the people about the right / responsibility of voting and participating in the democratic process?

_____

_____

_____

_____

_____

Seeing Faith

3. If our leaders and our governments are ordained by God, we should be praying for them! What are some specific prayers that we can pray for our country, our government and our leaders, by name. (Even the ones that we disagree with!)

_____

_____

_____

_____

_____

Pastor Jamie Ellis
Woodstation Church in Ringgold, Georgia

Seeing Faith
Political Service, Not for the Faint of Heart

I, like so many others, have wondered why are there not more good people serving politically.

I come from a family that has always been politically active. As a child, I helped to go door to door as my mother encouraged people to vote for a particular candidate she and my father were supporting. I have helped hand out buttons, stickers and everything in between.

In many communities, it is the voters themselves who are often doing the campaigning for the candidates, because it is simply an improbability for the candidate to reach each and every person's home.

After years of service to my community being a watchdog reporting upon the actions of government as a journalist, I decided to run for council in my hometown. I was honored to earn the trust and respect of the voters reflected through four elections.

I have worked with some talented, thoughtful people who have an earnest desire to see the community thrive in business development and prosper while fostering a sense of community among the residents and business owners.

Through community comes strength. Strength and success in business and in everyday pursuits and activities help to make the quality of life something to entice people and business to come to your town.

These things are often achieved through a process crafted by our founders called representative government. This process is sometimes referred to as a sausage factory. After

Seeing Faith

seeing it made, you are not as inclined to want to eat the sausage. Local elected officials who take what they are elected to do seriously will study through accredited classes, and learn their charter, the laws, the ordinances and the rules under which they govern. They seek to know what other similar cities are doing and often try to apply new ideas and approaches based on what they learn.

The purpose of local representative government is not to create harmony among the elected officials. It is to create a forum for the free exchange of ideas that streamline the operation of government and thus provide better, more economical services to its residents and businesses while helping to create economic growth to pay for those services.

In most cases, I have seen locally elected officials think through every action they take. The issues have been deliberated, financial aspects have been reviewed down to the penny sometimes for months and even years, and then when approved, it moves forward.

If an elected official is trying to do something, just one person does not do it. Instead, it is approved by the majority and then becomes the objective of all as the policy of the local government. You can bet your boots in most situations, even if some or a majority of elected officials oppose a motion, there is likely merit to what is trying to be accomplished.

Sadly, in many communities there are those who do not wish to see a community thrive. In fact, they desire to see people, initiatives or actions fail.

Armed with a misconception, an untruth taken out of context, or sometimes simply a lie about an action or an

Seeing Faith

inaction that has been reported inaccurately in media, social media, or by another authority of note, people proceed to spread the word about an elected or appointed official's actions without knowing, asking or understanding the purpose or intent.

We all do this. Often our frustration is aimed at people we will likely never meet, and have no way to watch the sausage being made at the national and state level.

In many cases the real problem is with all of us. We do not take the time to know what a wonderful opportunity our forefathers gave us with representative government. We do not take the time to go and watch the sausage being made even when it is produced in our own backyard. We would often rather stand at a distance, shake our heads, and spread a negative thought or deed rather than finding something good to share about what is happening in our community.

That is why more good people do not serve. Elected officials have to put on emotional armor as they hear and see their positive intentions twisted and turned for another's political benefit or someone's personal satisfaction. No matter how well intentioned, eventually the battle will grow heavy on those who have the kindest hearts, and they will grow weary and go home. They leave behind the politicians whose armor is strong enough to weather the attacks, and often their heart is hardened through the process. In some cases, the attacks do not phase the individual because they never cared about the office or the people who elected them anyway. Holding the office is simply a means to an unspoken end. Often these people are the authorities of note who privately or publically attack those doing actual good to

Seeing Faith

elevate their standing in the eyes of those less informed.

I would rather see my community represented by elected officials with a heart to serve who do not seek glory or recognition for their actions. Servants with open minds willing to listen, learn, and share their knowledge and experiences while sitting around a table and attempting to create a better tomorrow. But until we as people change our approach to representative government and realize that government is what we make it, especially at the local level, we will continue to chase away many of the best candidates and all they have to offer.

I applaud elected officials who can sustain with success in the light of the cruelty now fostered in our social-media-driven society.

Seeing Faith

Matthew 20:26-28

But it shall not be so among you: but whosoever will be great among you, let him be your minister; And whosoever will be chief among you, let him be your servant: Even as the Son of man came not to be ministered unto, but to minister, and to give his life a ransom for many.

John 13:14-15

If I then, your Lord and Master, have washed your feet; ye also ought to wash one another's feet. For I have given you an example, that ye should do as I have done to you.

Galatians 5:13

For, brethren, ye have been called unto liberty; only use not liberty for an occasion to the flesh, but by love serve one another.

1 Peter 4:10-11

As every man hath received the gift, even so minister the same one to another, as good stewards of the manifold grace of God. If any man speak, let him speak as the oracles of God; if any man minister, let him do it as of the ability which God giveth: that God in all things may be glorified through Jesus Christ, to whom be praise and dominion for ever and ever. Amen.

Seeing Faith

Leadership positions abound in the modern world, spanning every facet of life. Yet, amidst this abundance of leaders, only a few embody servant leadership. Servant leadership is not merely a label; it is a leadership model characterized by humility as the leader guides, mentors, and inspires those entrusted to their care. Servant leadership stands in stark contrast to the ego-driven pursuit of authority and personal gain. Instead, servant leadership embraces the discipline of placing the needs of others ahead of one's own desires and ambitions.

The foundation of servant leadership is based on love. Jesus said in John 13:34: "A new commandment I give unto you, That ye love one another; as I have loved you, that ye also love one another." The love for serving others is characteristic of Christ's love for us. The Apostle Paul, in his timeless epistle to the faithful congregation in Philippi, beckons believers to embrace the noble act of servant leadership, saying: "Let nothing be done through strife or vainglory; but in lowliness of mind let each esteem other better than themselves. Look not every man on his own things, but every man also on the things of others. Let this mind be in you, which was also in Christ Jesus" (Philippians 2:3-5). Thus, servant leadership is a call to selflessness, an invitation to mirror the character of Christ, who humbled Himself to the point of death on the cross for our sake (Philippians 2:8).

Humility is the true hallmark of servant leadership in any role of leadership. It is not merely a call for leaders to step forward but a profound invitation to embark on a journey to transform lives for the better.

Seeing Faith

1. The message highlights the challenges and opposition that can come with serving in local government and political leadership roles. How does the biblical principle of servant leadership, as exemplified by Jesus in passages like Matthew 20:26-28 and John 13:14-15, provide a contrasting model for those in positions of authority?

_____

_____

_____

_____

_____

2. The commentary emphasizes that servant leadership is rooted in love, humility, and selflessly putting others' needs above one's own desires, as instructed in verses like Philippians 2:3-5 and Galatians 5:13. How can cultivating this mindset help political leaders navigate the complexities and potential conflicts that arise in their roles?

_____

_____

_____

_____

_____

Seeing Faith

3. According to 1 Peter 4:10-11, believers are called to use their gifts in service to one another, as good stewards of God's grace. How might this principle apply to those serving in political or governmental roles, and how can they view their positions as an opportunity to minister and serve their communities?

_____

_____

_____

_____

_____

Dr. David Sampson
Parkway Baptist in Fort Oglethorpe, Georgia

Seeing Faith

Reaching Up from the Depths

Sometimes there are points in life when one reflects on topics that bring worry, sadness, concern or even depression.

They can pile up on our mind like leaves falling from the trees in autumn covering the roots that feed our soul.

Beneath the pile it gets hard to see a way out of the depths. Even the beauty of the arrival of spring or families gathering to celebrate the joy of days such as Easter, which normally should uplift our spirits, can also find a reason to weigh down upon the pile.

Randall Franks rakes leaves in his neighbor's yard in Atlanta, Ga.

I wish I could say, that it's a beautiful day, so go buy a rake and bag up the leaves, so the flowers that are emerging beneath the tree can shoot their blossoms up with greater ease. But oftentimes, we find that beneath the leaves the potential has withered due to the heavy covering.

It is in times like these that I must make an effort to connect even more to the roots beneath those leaves the people who care about me, and the Word of God which is the main food of my soul.

By engaging in the Word and in the lives of those around

Seeing Faith

me, especially those who need a helping hand, I find that I can breathe again, and the layers of sadness and concern seem to weigh less heavily. The problems that seemed so heavy are lightened when compared with the needs of others.

As I reach out to help, the worry that permeated each moment and seemed to take my breath is replaced by the effort to make a difference for others.

Sometimes when we feel like we are trapped down in the mine, the only way to feel less trapped is to join those who are trying to dig us out of the hole.

We can make a difference in the world even when we don't feel we can. In fact, sometimes we will find ourselves in the reactions and response of others as we work to make things better around us.

So head to the hardware store, buy a rake, a shovel, and anything else you need to make the world around you better and get to it.

You may find those heavy feelings replaced by hope, kindness and enthusiasm.

Seeing Faith

Hebrews 13:3
Remember them that are in bonds, as bound with them; and them which suffer adversity, as being yourselves also in the body.

"Reaching Up from the Depths" depicts a metaphorical picture of life's troubles and difficulties piling up like fallen leaves, weighing heavily and obscuring one's vision and hope. However, it suggests that by turning outward to engage with God's Word and extend compassion to those also experiencing adversity, as instructed in Hebrews 13:3, one can find renewed perspective and lightness of spirit. Just as the scripture urges remembering and identifying with the suffering of others, the message proposes that making an effort to alleviate others' burdens can paradoxically ease one's own sense of being trapped or overwhelmed. It portrays this outward focus and acts of service as providing hope, purpose, and a way to emerge from the depths of despondency. Thus, the message's encouragement to find renewed hope by remembering and aiding those facing hardship directly mirrors the teaching in Hebrews to empathize with and support those who are suffering or oppressed.

Seeing Faith

1. How can one show a Godly compassion to those in bonds or having adversity?

_____

_____

_____

_____

_____

2. How can one "remember" martyrs, veterans, widows, and orphans?

_____

_____

_____

_____

_____

3. *"Man can live ... only one second without hope"* **Hal Lindsey — How might one share hope with others?**

_____

_____

_____

_____

_____

Pastor Carroll Allen
Ringgold Church of God in Ringgold, Georgia

Seeing Faith
God Opens the Doors

It is amazing how God will open doors for people in their life. My road to Hollywood and network television is one He set in motion at an early age. I remember going to my mother and telling her "Mommy, I want to play my music on television like Flatt and Scruggs or The Darlings." She didn't discourage me; she just said, "We'll see what we can do."

Several years later, I had graduated and found myself coping with the news that my father Floyd, was diagnosed with lung cancer. He and my mother Pearl had been co-managing our youth group, The Peachtree Pickers.

The members of my group had all decided that with new responsibilities at college they needed to go a different direction. So I found myself at a reorganizing point once again after forming and reforming our group for several years encompassing 25 youth.

I was praying a lot over where the Lord wanted me to be musically. Should I bring together another band, go out as a soloist, or concentrate on finding a "real" job? Hearing the words that my dad, who was my constant companion on the road, especially since his retirement five years earlier, was threatened with facing this dreaded disease which could take him from mother and I spun me into an unusual merry-go-round of worry and denial of the danger.

God led me to walk through the doors of an acting course during this period. I had always loved being on stage and getting a chance to fulfill that childhood dream gave me a new focus for my energies.

Seeing Faith

I remember at one point that the doctors said, "With the treatments, he should have five more years."

Five more years, I thought, is not a lot, but it is in God's hands. While I sent up many prayers for Dad's healing. I distinctly remember one plea. I asked God these words: "God, if I am to do anything in television, please let it be in these next five years, so Dad may be part of it."

I made my first film appearance with a silent bit as a sports reporter in a movie to be called "Blind Side" starring John Beck and Gail Strickland that summer. I remember sitting at the kitchen table telling my mom and dad about my days on the set in the August heat on the football field. Just relaying the story, I could see a bit of enthusiasm return to Dad's face in spite of his declining condition.

It was just a couple more weeks before God chose to call Dad home.

But the story doesn't end there. That prayer I vocalized received an answer one year later, almost to the day when I received a call from casting director Dee Voight asking me to be on the set of a new television show that had moved to Georgia called "In the Heat of the Night" the next morning about 5:30.

I had seen the show's first episodes, and I remember saying, "If I am ever to be on television, this is the show." But how could that be? I was in Georgia and they were filming then in Louisiana, but God can make amazing things happen.

Dee wanted me to be on the set to perform as an extra in a crowd scene the first day of filming. I remember her saying, "I think they are going to like you." Within the first

Seeing Faith

hour one of the directors came by and said, "You look a lot like a police officer." I replied, "Thank you," not giving any thought to the work that God was doing behind the scenes. Over the next few weeks the directors kept bringing me back, using me as an extra on the show. Each time, even on that first day, I found myself in scenes doing silent bits with the stars of the show.

When about six weeks passed, they came to me and said that a new police character was to be added to the show and I was to be it. Within a very short time, "Officer Randy Goode" was born into a five-year role on NBC and CBS television. His gifts kept growing, bringing my work to new allies all the way up the studio and network ladder.

After being on the show for about a year, I realized I had reached part of that childhood goal, but as I found success in various areas being provided through God's love, in

Randall Franks leans against the exterior "In the Heat of the Night" set entrance to the Sparta Police Department in Covington, Georgia, in 1991.

prayer I asked God, "You are giving me all these wonderful opportunities, but what is it I am suppose to be here doing for you?"

Seeing Faith

A few weeks passed and I had my answer. I was called into the set through the echo of assistant directors fully expecting star and executive producer Carroll O'Connor to add me to a scene as he did many times before. Instead when I walked to the middle of the Chief's office and said "Yes, sir," Carroll looked at me and said, "I want to use a scripture in this scene."

Internally, I felt as if my mouth had dropped to the floor. About 100 people working for our show on the set and he called me in to give counsel about the first time that the "Chief Gillespie" would use a scripture that would touch the ears of more than 25 million Americans and millions of viewers in 150 countries around the world — many of whom never cross the threshold of a church door. I had never spoken to Carroll O'Connor about my faith, nor do I recall doing so with any that had his close counsel. I believe however that someone else whispered in his ear in answer to my prayer. We settled on I Corinthians 13:13, "And the greatest of these is charity," and that became his comment about the situation facing a young Vietnamese boy found needing help in our Sparta community in an episode entitled "My Name is Hank."

That began a wonderful dialogue between he and I on Christian and biblical topics. While not overly religious, the Chief Gillespie character became a purveyor of biblical wisdom through scriptures even leading a condemned prisoner to Christ in one episode.

Our characters sought inspiration and solace from God by attending church, we prayed before meals, sang songs of faith both on camera and in our CD "Christmas Time's A

Seeing Faith

Comin'" which God blessed me to produce featuring our entire cast and many notable guests. Executive producer Carroll O'Connor himself was seldom found from that point walking on the set without his script under one arm and a King James Bible beneath the other.

Carroll O'Connor, Lois Nettleton and Randall Franks on the set of "In the Heat of the Night"

This is a refreshing alternative to what we see on most gritty crime dramas, whether then or now. The show was unique and I thank God for allowing me to play a small part on the screen and off in its making.

By the way, God gave me another little gift before my departure from the show; many nice folks wrote in to our show about me and that encouraged Carroll O'Connor to write a scene that would feature me musically in an episode entitled "Random's Child." That childhood dream was reached.

God sows seeds in many gardens in hopes that one day they might bear great fruit. I was blessed to serve as one of His workers in this garden that fed and continues to feed millions 30-plus years later.

Seeing Faith
Notes

Seeing Faith

Proverbs 3:5-6
Trust in the LORD with all thine heart; And lean not unto thine own understanding. In all thy ways acknowledge him, And he shall direct thy paths.

This Christian walk we are on takes us through different terrains. The way might seem flat in one instance, and then take an uphill turn before you realize it. There are many twists and turns along the way. There are segments of the way where you may not even be able to see around the next corner. And that is exactly the point in our Christian walk where doubts and concerns seem to creep in. But we know that we walk by faith and not my sight. If we'll lean on the Word of God it will light our path.

1. Read Psalms 119:105. What is it that should provide light to the path ahead for the born again Christian?

_____

_____

_____

_____

Seeing Faith

2. What are some potential dangers of walking around in complete darkness? And how do they translate to the Christian absent the light of the Word of God.

_____

_____

_____

_____

_____

3. Look at 2 Corinthians 5:7 and Isaiah 46:10. Can you recall a time in your life when you couldn't see "around the next corner," yet God was faithful and His Word true? Do you think the situation you found yourself in caught our Lord God off guard?

_____

_____

_____

_____

_____

Assistant Pastor Mike Smith
Valley View Baptist Church in Flintstone, Georgia

Seeing Faith
Cleaning Out the Goop

I walked to the top of the ladder, climbed up on the roof, turned around and sat down looking down. I pulled another scoop of goop out of the gutter and placed it within the bucket I had hanging on the hook below me.

The long row of gutter ahead was scoop by scoop being cleaned out, and the bucket was filling up.

With every couple of scoops, I looked out upon the neighborhood, seeing it from a totally different vantage point. On one look up, I could see one neighbor cutting hedges with clippers while wearing a large triangle hat often seen in films of the far east. I watched a moment as she carefully sculpted the shape she desired. The care she placed in the task was evident.

I returned to my scooping, and soon my attention was grabbed as a lawn mower engine roared in another direction. Another neighbor in a T-shirt and a pair of overalls was riding his lawnmower, carefully creating diagonal lines, which shined in an amazing coordination from my view.

Far in the corner away from his work, his wife stood by the fence talking with a blonde lady in red exercise clothes who had stopped her walk.

I returned to my scooping as I inched foot by foot around the house until I spied two kids crossing the street. Across their shoulders were fishing poles, and in one of their hands was a string of fish they had pulled from the creek.

I returned to my scooping and soon I realized I had

Seeing Faith

matched my rhythm of work to a beating pattern which was coming from down the street. I looked closely to see what it was and I saw a group of kids were playing a game of basketball on a nearby driveway.

Once again, I returned to my scooping, and as I ended my task, I cleaned off the tools and disposed of the goop in the bucket in the trash can. As I prepared to shut the lid, a loud noise with no specific purpose except the deafening of those that could hear the sound of a bass that bounced from a car passed by.

I thought how the hour or so spent doing something productive allowed me to clear my mind of thoughts of everyday problems as I saw some of the best moments in my neighbors' lives. Did they see them as the best? Probably not. But within those moments, I saw people, living side by side, in all facets of everyday life from pure sport, intense horticulture hobbies, passing the time of day, to the victory of achieving one's goals. And like the departure of the raucous bass line as the vehicle cleared the neighborhood and the goop was tightly shut away in the waste bin, all was well in our world. And that is really what is important, how we are with one another in our neighborhood and our town. That is where we can make things better for all of us.

Seeing Faith

Romans 13:9
For this, Thou shalt not commit adultery, Thou shalt not kill, Thou shalt not steal, Thou shalt not bear false witness, Thou shalt not covet; and if there be any other commandment, it is briefly comprehended in this saying, namely, Thou shalt love thy neighbour as thyself.

Romans 13:10
Love worketh no ill to his neighbour: therefore love is the fulfilling of the law.

"Cleaning out the Goop" depicts a simple yet profound experience of cleaning out gutters on the roof and observing the everyday lives and activities of neighbors from this unique vantage point. It describes appreciating the small, sometimes overlooked moments that make up the fabric of a community — from gardening and yard work to children playing and passing conversations. This slice-of-life vignette reflects the scriptural teaching in Romans 13:9-10 about loving one's neighbor as oneself being the fulfillment of the law.

Seeing Faith

1. Do you know your neighbors?

_____

_____

_____

_____

_____

2. Have you showed the kindness and love of God to your neighbors?

_____

_____

_____

_____

_____

3. Do you think that social media has took away from the real social fabric our lives?

_____

_____

_____

_____

_____

Pastor Justin Gazaway
Catoosa Baptist Tabernacle in Ringgold, Georgia

Seeing Faith
The Freedom of Nothing Left to Prove

It seems so much of our life is spent working to prove something to someone else.

In our early years, we aspire to gain the approval of our parents or key mentors that wish to see us succeed in education, sports, music or whatever dream they hold for us or share with us.

Sometimes, it's the approval of our peers in these same pursuits, or other less beneficial objectives of youthful exuberance. There are those who succeed here and those who fail.

Often these successes or failures catapult our emotional make up forward, setting some of the undertones for our life. I know in my case, the failures left an underlying, "I'm going to show you" settled deep in my craw. I drew upon that hurt for many years, and it pushed me to overachieve in many ways.

No matter the outcome of youth, we step forward hoping to once again prove to the world that we can be somebody — a success in work, a success in picking the right person to marry, a success in raising children, a success in whatever is next on the long list that we seek others' approval to prop up our esteem, our importance, and our life.

Often we find ourselves in a cycle of seeking others' approval for the rest of our life.

In a conversation I was having with a friend the other day, I said something that I had not even thought about. As I look back upon the path I have traveled, I am blessed to

Seeing Faith

have had so many distinctive mentors to whom I have tried to prove my value in some aspect of my professional or personal endeavors.

As I began thinking, except in the form of being a creator of art in word, note and other form seeking the approval of those of you who buy my work and help me sustain the existence I enjoy, I thought I had no one left to prove anything to. Many of my key mentors who held those roles in my life have taken their final curtain calls.

As I relayed the story of a recent acting experience, I heard the words come out of my mouth, that I really wanted someone to acknowledge I could do what I was aspiring to do. I realized that I had not yet left behind that desire of proving something to someone. It was still buried inside me with one more youthful goal that had not been achieved in full but could still be accomplished if I tried hard enough. There it is driving me forward. After years of feeling I had nothing left to prove, which sometimes is not a bad place to be, once again, my blood is pumping with a desire, a hope, a goal that energizes my step.

So what is better, being to the point of nothing left to prove to anyone or having someone who inspires you to do more? I guess it depends on your own get up and go. I know one lady around 90 working on her doctorate. She has nothing to prove except to please her own soul.

If you are generally a self-starter, you probably move along OK, but every now and again, somebody may need to pour a little gasoline in your carburetor to get a spark and provide that forward momentum. If you need that in your life, I pray you have someone who provides that opportuni-

Seeing Faith

ty in love. Because in reality there are only two of us in this race to the finish line — us and the good Lord — who gives us a new chance every day to prove we are somebody serving, sharing and loving others for Him.

Seeing Faith

Psalm 25:9
The meek will he guide in judgment: and the meek will he teach his way.

Proverbs 11:2
When pride cometh, then cometh shame: but with the lowly is wisdom.

Proverbs 16:18
Pride goeth before destruction, and an haughty spirit before a fall.

Micah 6:8
He hath shewed thee, O man, what is good; and what doth the LORD require of thee, but to do justly, and to love mercy, and to walk humbly with thy God?

Matthew 23:12
And whosoever shall exalt himself shall be abased; and he that shall humble himself shall be exalted.

James 4:6
But he giveth more grace. Wherefore he saith, God resisteth the proud, but giveth grace unto the humble.

Seeing Faith

Within each of us, there exists a profound yearning to be cherished and loved. This longing is entirely natural, and it is a fundamental part of God's unique design of our humanity. However, as we navigate this desire, we must be cautious not to allow it to transform into an unhealthy craving for adoration. While it is honorable to strive for respect in our interactions with others, we must be cautious of the dangerous pitfall of craving selfish reverence. The perilous desire for excessive admiration is rooted in sinful pride, a trait that even transformed an angel into a devil (Isaiah 14:12-14, Ezekiel 28:12-18, Luke 10:18). The angel Lucifer's heart became consumed with a sinful desire to showcase his own glory, a yearning that negated his devotion to the Sovereign Creator. This sin of pride transformed this once-glorious angel into a devil, the embodiment of sinful rebellion. The consequences of Lucifer's sinful actions were severe, leading to his expulsion from the heavenly abode and sealing his fate with a pending judgment from God Himself. His tragic fall serves as a solemn reminder of the dangers of allowing pride to overshadow our devotion to God's glory.

Our attitude should reflect the desire of John the Baptist who said: "He must increase, but I must decrease" (John 3:30). Living a life that glorifies God is a profound journey characterized by humility that will result in spiritual maturity and blessings. Jesus said, "But seek ye first the kingdom of God, and his righteousness; and all these things shall be added unto you" (Matthew 6:33). Our primary quest should be aligning ourselves with God's kingdom agenda, and in doing so, we can rest assured that God will fulfill His

Seeing Faith

promise and provide for our need.

1. The message reflects on the human desire to prove oneself and gain the approval of others, whether parents, mentors, or peers. However, the commentary warns against allowing this desire to become an unhealthy craving for excessive admiration rooted in sinful pride, using the example of Lucifer's fall. How can we strike the proper balance between having healthy goals/aspirations while guarding against the pitfalls of pride?

_____

_____

_____

_____

_____

Seeing Faith

2. Both the message and the commentary emphasize the importance of humility and focusing on serving God rather than seeking glory for oneself (John 3:30, Matthew 6:33). What practical steps can we take to cultivate an attitude of humility and a desire to exalt Christ rather than ourselves in our various pursuits and relationships?

_____

_____

_____

_____

_____

3. The scriptures provided (e.g., Proverbs 11:2, 16:18, Matthew 23:12) clearly outline the dangers and consequences of pride, contrasting it with the blessings that come from walking humbly with God. How can meditating on and applying these verses help to guard our hearts against the temptation of pride and keep us rooted in a posture of humility?

_____

_____

_____

_____

_____

Dr. David Sampson
Parkway Baptist in Fort Oglethorpe, Georgia

Seeing Faith
Notes

Seeing Faith
The Needle Is Stuck Again

I have seen numerous members of my family and friends go through the ups and downs of chronic illnesses, and watched as they struggled with tasks which once they had performed with ease.

© 1976 Randall Franks Media – Randall Franks

Georgia McMahan

When I was just a child volunteering in a local nursing home, I met a woman who was around eighty at the time. Her name was Georgia McMahan. Georgia endured many of the ailments of her fellow residents but you would never know it.

From the moment you saw her, the smile that beamed from her face uplifted you and gave you a spirit of glee that could carry you through any task. Added to the smile were words of encouragement, concern, and hope that poured from her very being.

While many of the folks that my efforts brought me in contact with were mired in what seem to be a ditch of despair, Georgia shined as if standing on a mountaintop in a field of wild flowers.

Sometimes as I hear different people share similar issues again and again, I see in my mind the spinning turntable of

Seeing Faith

my youth with a 33 1/3 rpm record going round and round. I remember when a particular tune had been played too much or accidently scratched, sometimes the needle would find itself stuck and repeat the same musical phrase over and over again.

It took me getting up, going to the record player, and bumping the needle's arm ever so gently to help it get out of the record's deep dark vinyl groove and move it musically on down the road.

Like that needle, it is so easy to get stuck in the scratches and worn out spaces of our lives and find it hard to move on. We spin around endlessly in the same spot, repeating the same actions, saying the same things only to find ourselves doing it over again.

Sometimes it takes someone to give us a gentle shove to realize that just a millimeter down our path we may find something better, and even if we don't, we are better for the trying.

As I think back on Georgia now, I sort of see her as that person in that place who God sent to gently nudge all those around her and give them a chance to stop being stuck in a groove that was wearing on them and everyone that could hear their song.

Are you serving as a catalyst to help yourself and others over the hump and find a smoother path? If not, why not? I can surely say the path that Georgia showed me as a child sure gives life a better spin than any others I have seen. I hope I can always take the spin that lets me seem as if I am on the mountain in a field of wildflowers.

Seeing Faith

2 Corinthians 1:3
Blessed be God, even the Father of our Lord Jesus Christ, the Father of mercies, and the God of all comfort;

2 Corinthians 1:4
Who comforteth us in all our tribulation, that we may be able to comfort them which are in any trouble, by the comfort wherewith we ourselves are comforted of God.

Have you ever wondered why God sometimes allows us to get stuck in a proverbial rut? Just as Randall's story suggests, we all seem to have our spiritual needles caught in that endless groove of life. In many cases it takes someone else outside our circumstances to give us a little nudge to get our life's song progressing again. I have always been intrigued by the notion of "pay it forward". Someone might buy your lunch or pay for your groceries and then ask you to "pay it forward" to someone else. This is exactly what we should do spiritually in God's economy according to 2 Corinthians 1:3-4. God allows us to go thru certain uncomfortable times so that we can know what others are going thru and comfort them in their time of need. Have you been through some hard times in life's record groove? Then look for someone else's needle that needs a little nudge.

Seeing Faith

1. What are the most difficult problems that you have faced in life?

_____

_____

_____

_____

_____

2. Is there anyone you know who might be experiencing some of the same problems you have? Have you thought of giving them a call, sending them a letter in the mail, or visiting them?

_____

_____

_____

_____

_____

Seeing Faith

3. Did you know that there is no problem you have ever faced or will ever face that someone else has not faced already? See 1 Corinthians 10:13.

_____

_____

_____

_____

_____

Pastor Jeff Brown
Valley View Baptist Church in Flintstone, Georgia

Seeing Faith
Notes

Seeing Faith
Is There Light at the End of the Tunnel?

There are not many instances that we today have an application for such a question. Tunnels are few and far between in our day-to-day travels unless you live where subways or mountain tunnels are the norm.

I can remember as a boy walking through an abandoned railroad tunnel and becoming so very aware at how dark the tunnel is once you leave the light of the opening. With each step I found my trip even more tenuous as I stumbled over fallen bricks and rocks. Even as I lay flat on my stomach with my face in the dirt, I remember trying to look forward to see if there was light at the end of the tunnel.

That darkness only becomes deeper the further you walk away from the light, but if you walk far enough down the tunnel (assuming that it is not a dead end), you will eventually once again come to the light and find an opportunity to leave the darkness behind.

It's a safe bet that every human being on earth has metaphorically endured this same experience in some part of their life. Whether by their own choices or by the actions of another, you feel like you are walking down that darkened path that seems to lead only to darker shadows.

You stumble, you fall, you get up, and you try harder to make your way through the darkness only to repeat the process again when you once again can't find the way out on your own. Then eventually in the distance the Light shines through and you race towards it hopeful that you will never find yourself in such a place again.

Once in the Light though, it is easy to forget the dark-

Seeing Faith

ness and the trials endured and once again stumble away from the Light into the place you never wanted to be again. What is amazing though is the Light is always there to shine on a path to give us the opportunity to come through the trial.

Once through, if we rely totally on the Light, maybe we will never need to seek the light at the end of tunnel again.

Seeing Faith

John 8:12
**Then spake Jesus again unto them, saying, I am the
light of the world: he that followeth me shall not walk
in darkness, but shall have the light of life.**

In the New Testament, the Greek word "Peripateo" is
the word that is translated as "walk". In the original language it more closely means, "walking around in". It is
NOT moving with a purpose, but very descriptively
describes someone that is walking around in darkness. No
direction. No understanding of where they should be. Lost.
Before answering these questions, I invite you to close your
eyes and place yourself in that tunnel. To wonder how long
the darkness lasts…to feel stones and sticks beneath your
feet and to feel the isolation and fear that comes with the
unknown.

Seeing Faith

1. Read Isaiah 9:2 (The people that walked in darkness have seen a great light: they that dwell in the land of the shadow of death, upon them hath the light shined.) In what ways does Jesus fulfill the prophetic words of Isaiah?

_____

_____

_____

_____

_____

2. In your life, what periods of darkness have you experienced? In what ways has Christ delivered you from that darkness?

_____

_____

_____

_____

_____

Seeing Faith

3. What are some things that you can do to bring the light of Christ into the lives of others who are still in the darkness?

_____

_____

_____

_____

_____

Pastor Jamie Ellis
Woodstation Church in Ringgold, Georgia

Seeing Faith
Notes

Seeing Faith
The Mirror Reflects Only What It Sees

Many of us find ourselves each morning at least for a few minutes peering into a silver backed piece of glass which reflects back towards us the mirror image of ourselves.

We see the teeth as we brush, the pores of our skin as we wash our face, shave, and or trim the hairs which grew out since the day before. Finally, we put each hair left on top of our head in place with a comb or a brush.

Then off we go to dress, and we pop back in for one last look before we run off to meet the day and all that entails.

As the day progresses, we will stop by other bathrooms like a racing car making a pit stop, and once again we will have a moment to peer into the silver-backed glass to see if all is still in its proper place.

These are rituals that we have been taught from parents, siblings, and friends, and they are common to most human beings who have access to such an opportunity.

As a child, at amusement parks and fairs, I can remember going through a house of mirrors that distorted the mirror image to make one look short or tall, skinny or fat, oddly shaped in all forms and sizes. It was always a laugh to see yourself or your companions going through the metamorphosis of illusions that the fun house mirrors reflected.

The present-day mirror was brought to us from the work of German chemist Justus von Liebig about 180 years ago. For years, human beings found the looking glass a means of self-discovery.

I have often heard people say something to the effect of

Seeing Faith

"You won't be able to look at yourself in the morning." I really wonder how many of us take that to heart.

Have you ever really looked in a mirror and tried to see beyond the superficial image of yourself staring back?

Have you tried to look down into your own heart, soul and mind to see if what is reflected upon that image is something you really want to see or you want others to see of you?

We all have blemishes, scars, warts, sores and sometimes wounds that can be seen when we look close enough that we want to cover over and hide from the outside world. No matter how much concealer is used, they eventually rise to the surface trying to once again draw attention.

I guess no matter how hard we try, we must learn to live with those and become comfortable in our own skin, allowing all those imperfections not to bother us or anyone else. God did not create vessels of perfection in human beings. He created people who have the opportunity to strive for perfection despite the brokenness within their lives and their souls.

The image in the mirror will never be perfect. To strive for that is an exercise in vanity, but to use the mirror to step closer to internal perfection might be an interesting step into the looking glass.

Seeing Faith

James 1:23-24
For if any be a hearer of the word, and not a doer, he is like unto a man beholding his natural face in a glass: For he beholdeth himself, and goeth his way, and straightway forgetteth what manner of man he was.

Seeking one' heart, soul and mind when facing one's reflection, "The Mirror Reflects Only What It Sees" challenges us to look more deeply into transforming our inner lives, when often we focus exclusively upon our external selves.

The message reflects this scriptural analogy by encouraging introspection beyond one's outward appearance when looking in the mirror. Just as James warns against merely glancing at one's reflection and immediately forgetting one's true nature, the message exhorts readers to peer deeper than the superficial image. It acknowledges how we often focus on grooming our external selves while ignoring or concealing internal "blemishes, scars, and wounds" that need attention. The implicit suggestion is to use the mirror as a prompt for self-examination and growth, rather than dwelling solely on outward appearances. This aligns with

Seeing Faith

James' contrast between the forgetful glancer who remains unchanged and the substantive "doer" who applies the wisdom gained from truly beholding themselves. By posing questions about genuinely seeing into one's heart, soul and mind when facing one's reflection, the message challenges the tendency to be mere "hearers" who overlook opportunities for transformation.

1. When looking in the mirror, what specific internal qualities or areas of growth do you need to give more attention to, rather than just your outward appearance?

_____

_____

_____

_____

_____

2. How can the daily ritual of grooming in front of a mirror become an opportunity for introspection and intentional self-improvement, as this passage encourages?

_____

_____

_____

_____

_____

Seeing Faith

3. Beyond just ourselves, how can we encourage friends, family or others around us to look past superficial reflections and address deeper matters of the heart, soul and mind?

_____

_____

_____

_____

_____

Seeing Faith
Notes

Seeing Faith
The Loss of History Dooms Our Future

As we worked in the recording studio, the nearby fireworks popped and boomed in the sky nearby.

After a 10-hour day in the studio of producing the amazing talents of a group of youth bringing together some original music to share to radio, my mind set back to the coming day ahead — Independence Day.

In our family, the day always marked my late mother's birth, now 98 years earlier, but my folks never let me forget that it stood for something so much more when a group of American patriots gathered, debated, and ultimately signed a document to cut our colonial ties with England, beginning years of war.

For most of these men, it meant loss, hardships and an uncertain future, but because they made the choice, our country was set on a path to freedom. Forty eight of these 56 men were part of my extended family.

We are still a young country in the realm of our world's history, yet in recent years, it seems many people and groups they align with spend a lot of time reframing history to reflect the lense of today's experience and thinking.

Overseas under the cloud that has risen the last two decades, we have seen terrorists destroy historical places, statues, and artifacts, because those that created them did not align with their beliefs. Thousands of years wiped from the face of the earth because of the thoughts of someone today with no respect for those who came before or a desire to learn from their existence.

They judge the actions and thoughts of those set in a

Seeing Faith

different time and place and often in a world we could not even envision living within, condemning them for their place in history sometimes on one aspect of their choices within the bounds of the society in which they survived.

Generations of our ancestors lived in a world in which slavery was the norm. In fact many of our own ancestors were slaves at some point, whether they were sold into slavery for profit or as the spoils of victory between warring peoples, were born as a serf spending their life toiling for a royal land owner, or became an indentured servant to work off a debt or secure something better years in to the future.

In reality, today, there are millions of our brothers and sisters living around the world who are toiling in slavery, with their lives bartered and sold at the whims of others. Sadly, this is true even within the shadows in our present day America, inside the norms of certain cultures, and in the sex trafficking trade.

Many of us have seen the news or historical reports of millions of people killed in places around the world in an effort to end the existence of a race or tribe of people, a group of people who worship in a particular religion, or people with a different political ideology and national allegiance.

Even within our short-lived history in America, our ancestors have fought wars, skirmishes and battles to win the American continent. They fought native indigenous people and other European powers that dominated various regions. They took public policies on our own soil, that resulted in certain people following particular religions,

Seeing Faith

being or certain race or nationality being persecuted or not given equal opportunities.

So, some activists choose to wipe out the admiration and acknowledgement of millions of past Americans for the contributions of presidents, governors, legislators, scholars, educators, explorers, statesmen, military officers, and just plain folks because they condemn where that person fell on an issue, belief, political alliance or life choice. Unfortunately, now, many have found themselves in positions of power, whether elected, appointed or hired, and they bow to the loud voices of the present ignoring the voices of the millions who came before and choosing to hide away our history. However, in their time they worked and raised monies to erect statues and place monuments to people that moved or changed the world in a positive way for their time.

As a result, we have seen statues moved, monuments destroyed, plaques taken down. At least in our country the activists have not taken on the 'let's blow it to kingdom come' approach we have seen of some of our world's greatest treasures overseas.

If we revise the visual depictions of our past and hide away the people who made it to suit our present perspectives, how will we learn from past mistakes? Our world and all aspects of the human experience were brought forward by flawed individuals. It's by examining their experiences, their flaws from the modern-day lense, that we are not doomed to repeat the history they experienced. But if we tear down our past, we are simply setting ourselves up for more of the same. Learn from those who came before.

Seeing Faith

Don't judge their actions based on where we are.

If you want to fix something, the same atrocities from the past exist today... Fix that. If you look close enough, there is a living, breathing person who is within your midst who needs the attention to change their life and circumstances. Spend your energies on fixing that, rather than trying to win a victory over those who can no longer speak for themselves.

Seeing Faith

Proverbs 22:28
Remove not the ancient landmark,
which thy fathers have set.

"The Loss of History Dooms Our Future's" concern over the revisionism and erasure of history directly mirrors the wisdom expressed in Proverbs 22:28 about not removing the ancient landmarks set by previous generations. It decries the contemporary practice of judging the thoughts and actions of ancestors through an isolated modern lens, failing to consider the realities and norms of their era. This modern inclination to condemn the past and destroy its remnants is viewed as a destructive loss of the ability to learn from history's lessons — akin to violating the scriptural exhortation against removing the landmarks established by one's forebearers. The examples of terrorists demolishing ancient sites, civilizations persecuting groups, and America's own complex heritage with slavery and conflicts are portrayed, as critical parts of the human story that should be preserved and contextualized, not erased. The overarching idea is that rejecting the ancestral "landmarks" of history strips humanity of vital wisdom and forecloses understanding, aligning with Proverbs' caution about tampering with the foundations laid by previous generations.

Seeing Faith

1. How is our present-day culture removing our historical and Biblical landmarks?

_____

_____

_____

_____

_____

2. What purpose did the 12 stones serve in the midst of the Jordan River (Joshua 4:9)?

_____

_____

_____

_____

_____

3. Why is it important to obey the voice of God, as Noah?

_____

_____

_____

_____

_____

Pastor Carroll Allen
Ringgold Church of God in Ringgold, Georgia

Seeing Faith

Seeing Faith

Seeing Faith

Actor/entertainer Randall Franks is best known as "Officer Randy Goode" from TV's "In the Heat of the Night," a role he performed on NBC and CBS from 1988–1993. A star of UPtv from 2009–2014, he appeared in several films and with Robert Townsend in the series "Musical Theater of Hope."

He has co-starred or starred in 20 films with superstars including Dolly Parton, Christian Slater, William Hurt, Stella Parton, and legendary western star "Doc" Tommy Scott. His most recent film is "The Cricket's Dance"

Randall Franks

with Kristen Renton, Maurice Johnson, William Mark McCullough and Sandra Ellis Lafferty.

Franks' musical stylings have been heard in 150 countries and by more than 25 million Americans. The Independent Country Music Hall of Fame member's musical career boasts 25 album releases, 21 singles, and over 200 recordings with artists from various genres. The International Bluegrass Music Hall of Fame Legend annually hosts the historic Grand Master Fiddler Championship for several years at the Country Music Hall of Fame and Museum in Nashville, Tenn. The award-winning fiddler's best-selling release, "Handshakes and Smiles," was a top twenty Christian music seller. Many of his albums were among the top 30 bluegrass recordings of their release year. The Atlanta Country Music Hall of Fame member shared a top country vocal collaboration with Grand Ole Opry stars the Whites. In addition to his solo performances, tours with his Hollywood Hillbilly Jamboree, and years of guest starring for the Grand Ole Opry, Franks is a former member of Bill Monroe's Blue Grass Boys and Jim and Jesse's Virginia Boys. He has performed with Jeff and Sheri Easter, the Lewis Family, the Marksmen Quartet, the Watkins Family, Elaine and Shorty, "Doc" Tommy Scott's Last Real Old Time Medicine Show, and Doodle and the Golden River Grass.

Seeing Faith

He is the former Vice Mayor and Council Chairman in Ringgold, Ga., and is Catoosa Citizens for Literacy chairman, which assists individuals in learning to read and pursuing a GED at its Catoosa County Learning Center near Ringgold. He is also president of the Share America Foundation, Inc. that provides the Pearl and Floyd Franks Scholarship to musicians continuing the traditional music of Appalachia. He is the Northwest Georgia Joint Economic Development Authority film industry liaison. He is the Georgia Production Partnership past vice president and serves on government relations.

He authored ten other books, including "Testing the Metal of Life: The Joe Barger Story" with Joe Barger, "A Badge or an Old Guitar: A Music City Murder Mystery;" "Encouragers I: Finding the Light;" "Encouragers II: Walking with the Masters;" "Encouragers III: A Guiding Hand;" "Whittlin' and Fiddlin' My Own Way: The Violet Hensley Story" with Violet Hensley; "A Mountain Pearl: Appalachian Reminiscing and Recipes;" "Stirring Up Success with a Southern Flavor," and "Stirring Up Additional Success with a Southern Flavor" with Shirley Smith; and "Snake Oil, Superstars and Me" with "Doc" Tommy Scott and Shirley Swiesz.

A journalist with more than 20 state and national awards, Franks is also a syndicated columnist with his "Southern Style" appearing weekly in newspapers from North Carolina to Texas and at randallfranks.com. He was included among his generation's leading country humorists in the Loyal Jones book "Country Music Humorists and Comedians."

For more information, visit www.randallfranks.com and www.shareamericafoundation.org.

Be sure to visit on the web:
Randall Franks on X
https://twitter.com/RandallFranks
Randall Franks Fan Page on Facebook
www.facebook.com/RandallFranksActorDirectorEntertainer
Randall Franks on YouTube:
http://www.youtube.com@randallfranks
Randall Franks at IMDB:
http://www.imdb.com/name/nm0291684/

Randall Franks (left) as "Capt. Robert Shields" in "The American's Creed"
Learn more and Get the Film and Documentary at
www.RandallFranks.com/The-Americans-Creed

Seeing Faith

About Our Contributing Pastors

Provided by the Pastors

PASTOR CARROLL ALLEN

South Georgia native, Bishop Alton Carroll Allen, is married to Donna, and is a seasoned pastor/evangelist. He is presently at his second Georgia pastorate at the Ringgold Church of God since April 2001.

PASTOR JEFF BROWN

Pastor Jeff "Jabo" Brown was saved at the age of 24 years old and called to preach at the age of 33. He is now 53 years old and the senior pastor at Valley View Baptist Church in Flintstone, Georgia. He is married to his beautiful wife of 28 years, Belinda Brown, and has a wonderful and musically talented son named Colton Brown who is 21 years of age. Pastor Jeff received his secular education from the University of Tennessee at Chattanooga and his Biblical education from Gulf Coast Bible Institute in Ft. Walton Beach, Florida.

REVEREND CHRIS BRYANT

The Rev. Chris Bryant is an ordained elder in the United Methodist Church and has been a pastor since 1996. He and his wife Kara have five boys between them and currently reside in Ringgold, Georgia.

Seeing Faith
Contributing Pastors

REVEREND JAMIE ELLIS, MDiv, ThM, PhD

Pastor Jamie Ellis is a Hospice Chaplain and the Pastor of Woodstation Church, an Independent Church in the Wesleyan Tradition. He graduated From Lakeview Fort Oglethorpe High School in North Georgia. After high school he earned degrees from Dalton State College, University of Tennessee, Chattanooga, Golden Gate Baptist Theological Seminary, and completed a Clinical Pastoral Education Residency with Erlanger Hospital. In his ministry career he has served as an Air Force Chaplain as well as Youth Minister, Chaplain in both Hospitals and Hospice. He is married to Kerri Ellis and they have two kids, Blane and Harper as well as a daughter in law Tatianna.

PASTOR JUSTIN GAZAWAY

Pastor Justin Gazaway is the senior pastor of Catoosa Baptist Tabernacle since 2016. Prior to his service at CBT, Justin pastored Cloverleaf Baptist Church for 13 years in Cartersville, Georgia.

Seeing Faith
Contributing Pastors

PASTOR DAVID SAMPSON

Dr. David Sampson serves as the Senior Pastor of Parkway Baptist located in Fort Oglethorpe, Georgia. He holds a Bachelor of Theology, a Master of Pastoral Theology, and a Doctor of Ministry from Liberty University, as well as a Doctorate in Theological Studies from Andersonville Theological Seminary. With over 30 years of experience in preaching ministry, Dr. Sampson brings a wealth of knowledge and dedication to his role. Alongside his wife, Melissa, they are natives of Northwest Indiana and proud parents to three children and grandparents to several grandchildren.

ASSISTANT PASTOR MIKE SMITH

Assistant Pastor Mike Smith is born again through his faith in the death, burial, and resurrection of Jesus Christ. He believes his King James Bible is the complete Word of God, the final and sole authority on all matters of faith and practice. He is currently enrolled in the Gulf Coast Bible Institute and serving as Assistant Pastor at Valley View Baptist Church in Flintstone, Georgia. He is the husband of a beautiful wife, Whitney, and two wonderful children, Josie and Penton.

Seeing Faith Index

The index does not include Jesus and the author, who are mentioned throughout the book.

Seeing Faith Index

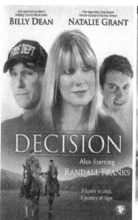  

Buy Other Books by
Randall Franks

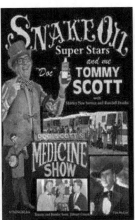

A Mountain Pearl : Appalachian Reminiscing and Recipes
Whittlin' and Fiddlin' My Own Way : The Violet Hensley Story
Testing the Metal of Life : The Joe Barger Story
Stirring Up Success with a Southern Flavor

www.RandallFranks.com/Store

https://www.amazon.com/stores/Randall-Franks/author/B00K9XIDN4